3

re to L
last

POCKET
DICTIONARY *of*
APOLOGETICS
& PHILOSOPHY
OF RELIGION

C. STEPHEN EVANS

InterVarsity Press
Downers Grove, Illinois
Leicester, England

InterVarsity Press
P.O. Box 1400, Downers Grove, IL 60515-1426, USA
World Wide Web: www.ivpress.com
E-mail: mail@ivpress.com

Inter-Varsity Press, England
38 De Montfort Street, Leicester LE1 7GP, England
World Wide Web: www.ivpbooks.com
E-mail: ivp@uccf.org.uk

InterVarsity Press®, U.S.A., is the book-publishing division of InterVarsity Christian Fellowship/USA®, a student movement active on campus at hundreds of universities, colleges and schools of nursing in the United States of America, and a member movement of the International Fellowship of Evangelical Students. For information about local and regional activities, write Public Relations Dept., InterVarsity Christian Fellowship/USA, 6400 Schroeder Rd., P.O. Box 7895, Madison, WI 53707-7895, or visit the IVCF website at <www.ivcf.org>.

Inter-Varsity Press, England, is the book-publishing division of the Universities and Colleges Christian Fellowship (formerly the Inter-Varsity Fellowship), a student movement linking Christian Unions in universities and colleges throughout the United Kingdom and the Republic of Ireland, and a member movement of the International Fellowship of Evangelical Students. For information about local and national activities write to UCCF, 38 De Montfort Street, Leicester LE1 7GP.

Scripture quotations, unless otherwise noted, are from the New Revised Standard Version of the Bible, copyright 1989 by the Division of Christian Education of the National Council of the Churches of Christ in the USA. Used by permission. All rights reserved.

Cover illustration: Roberta Polfus

ISBN 0-8308-1465-5

UK ISBN 0-85111-263-3

Printed in the United States of America ∞

Library of Congress Cataloging-in-Publication Data

Evans, C. Stephen.
  Pocket dictionary of apologetics & philosophy of religion/C. Stephen Evans.
    p. cm.
  ISBN 0-8308-1465-5 (pbk.: alk. paper)
  1. Religion—Philosophy—Dictionaries. 2. Apologetics—Dictionaries. I. Title: Pocket dictionary of apologetics and philosophy of religion. II. Title.
  BL51 .E863 2002
  210'.3—dc 21   *2001051597*

British Library Cataloguing in Publication Data

A catalogue record for this book is available from the British Library.

16	15	14	13	12	11	10	9	8	7	6	5	4	3	2	1
15	14	13	12	11	10	09	08	07	06	05	04	03	02		

Preface

It is an interesting time for a Christian to work in the philosophy of religion. When I went to graduate school in 1969, the number of Christians in philosophy was small and their influence smaller. I have been privileged to live through a period in which God has called a number of people to work in this vineyard. One evidence of this is the fact that the Society of Christian Philosophers currently has over twelve hundred members on its rolls. Philosophy of religion and apologetics seem to be flourishing in ways that would have been unthinkable fifty years ago.

Much of the work that has been done in this area is potentially of great interest to educated Christian laypeople in many fields. Philosophy of religion and apologetics, however, like many fields, have their own specialized jargon that can make it difficult for the nonspecialist to follow the writings. This little dictionary attempts to define some of the key terms needed to understand the philosophers and theologians writing in this area. I have made every effort to be concise and clear. In some cases, though, I do go beyond simple definitions to offer minimal accounts of the important issues. While I am sure my biases will show, and while the book is clearly written from the perspective of one committed to the historic Christian faith, I have attempted to be fair with respect to controversial issues, particularly where there is disagreement among Christians.

This work was inspired by the *Pocket Dictionary of Theological Terms*, and I wish to thank Stanley Grenz, David Guretzki and Cherith Fee Nordling both for the model they provided in that book and for their insight with respect to some of the overlapping terms. I have followed the format of their work, with all terms, phrases and names arranged in alphabetical order. I have, however, elected to include more proper names than might be expected in a dictionary, since I believe that an understanding of apologetics and philosophy of religion requires an understanding of the work of important philosophers and theologians, both classical and contemporary.

In a reference work like this a system of cross-references is invaluable. An asterisk before a term or phrase indicates that it appears elsewhere in the book as a separate entry. *See* and *see also* references direct readers to entries that provide additional information.

I hope and pray that this work will be of use to those interested in serious thinking about religious and theological issues, especially those who are part of God's church. In my own attempt at apologetics—*Why Believe?*—I caution against overestimating the importance of apologetics. I do not believe all Christians must explore such issues in order to have a reasonable faith in God as revealed in Jesus of Nazareth. I am convinced, however, that hard, honest thought about what Christians believe and why can be of great benefit to the church, and I will be delighted if this book contributes to that goal in a modest way.

C. Stephen Evans

A

a posteriori, a priori. Terms used to describe the logical status of propositions and arguments with respect to their dependence upon, or independence from, sense experience. An a posteriori proposition is one that is known on the basis of sense experience. An a priori proposition is one that can be determined to be true independently of sense experience. Most philosophers agree that analytic propositions such as "All bachelors are unmarried" can be known a priori, because their truth cannot be affected by any empirical observations. However, the status of mathematical and metaphysical propositions (such as "Whatever has a beginning has a cause") is debated.

Abelard, Peter (1079-1142). French Scholastic philosopher and theologian who made important contributions to logic and philosophy of language, and offered notable explications of such Christian doctrines as the *Trinity and the *atonement. Abelard is also famous for a celebrated, tragic love affair with Héloïse (c. 1117). He was the first Western medieval philosopher to make use of *Aristotle's *On Interpretation*.

action (divine and human). A special type of event originated by persons understood as "agents," that is, conscious beings with intentions. Thus, when the event that constitutes my arm being raised is brought about by my raising my arm, the change constitutes an act or action. (Having one's arm raised against one's will by a rope attached to it would not constitute an action.) Many actions are performed by doing other actions. For example, I turn on the light by flipping the switch. However, not all actions are of this sort; some are "basic actions," since if I must always perform one action to carry out another, an infinite regress would ensue. Philosophers debate whether basic actions are a type of bodily movement or whether such bodily movements are the result of something still more basic—a volition or mental act of willing. Actions are typically done for a reason, and there is also controversy as to how actions are to be explained. Are reasons to be understood as causes? Debate also rages as to whether all actions are causally determined. (*See* determinism; free will.) To think of God as a personal agent is to attribute to God the power to act as well. Debates here link up with disputes about whether God is atemporal or everlasting; does God do all he does in one eternal action, or is he capable of sequential acts? (*See* eternity/everlasting.) How are God's actions related to the divine will and intellect? God's actions must be understood in relation to *creation and *providence and in connection with special acts such as *miracles. *See also* divine action.

Advaita Vedanta. A nondualistic form of Hindu theology, or Vedanta. According to Advaita Vedanta, ultimate reality is one—the absolute divine unity of Brahman that is beyond description in language. The human soul, or Atman, is identical with this absolute reality, and enlightenment or deliverance involves a realization of this oneness. At the level of appearance, objects in the world seem to be distinct from such things as the self and a personal deity. According to Advaita Vedanta, the sacred Hindu writings the Upanishads teach that such distinctions are not metaphysically ultimate. *See also* Hinduism; monism.

afterlife. *See* life after death.

agapism. A type of ethical tradition that centers on the Christian understanding of *love as *agape* (self-giving love of the "neighbor") in distinction from *philia* (friendship love) and *eros* (love involving desire, such as romantic love). Agapism focuses on the great love commandments of Matthew 22:37-40 as well as the centrality of love in other New Testament writings. Though there is a long tradition of Christian reflection on this theme, Anders Nygren's *Agape and Eros* (1930) is a seminal, though much-criticized, twentieth-century presentation of agapism in *ethics.

agnosticism. The position that neither affirms belief in God (*theism) nor denies the existence of God (*atheism) but instead suspends judgment. It is helpful to distinguish the "modest agnostic," who merely claims to be unable to decide the question of God's reality, from the "aggressive agnostic," who claims that no one can decide the question and that suspension of judgment is the only reasonable stance. *See also* belief; doubt.

Alston, William (1921-). North American Christian philosopher who has done important work in *epistemology, philosophy of language, philosophy of perception and *philosophy of religion. Alston was part of the group (along with Alvin *Plantinga and Nicholas *Wolterstorff) that developed *Reformed Epistemology. He was also the prime mover behind the founding of the Society of Christian Philosophers. He served as the first president of that organization as well as the first editor of its journal, *Faith and Philosophy.*

analogical predication. Language used to describe God that is between *univocal language, in which terms applied to two or more objects have precisely the same sense, and *equivocal language, in which the same term is applied to two or more things in completely unrelated senses. Philosophers such as Thomas *Aquinas have claimed that positive language derived from our experience of the finite world cannot be applied univocally to God but that terms such as "goodness" and "knowledge" can be applied analogically to God, meaning that God possesses in an unrestricted fashion the perfections the terms designate.

analogy of being. The view that, though God is infinite and the created world is finite, the being of the world reflects enough of its Creator so that the language used to describe it can be applied analogically to God. This view is usually associated with philosophical arguments for the existence of God. (*See* theistic arguments.) The analogical similarity is usually thought to be particularly valid for human beings since they are created in the *image of God. The analogy of being has been rejected by Karl *Barth and others who are critical of *natural theology. *See also* analogical predication.

analogy of faith. The view that interpretation of the Scriptures should be governed by *faith. For *Augustine, this meant that the Scriptures should be interpreted in terms of the "rule of faith"—the teachings of the church as embedded in the creeds. For Martin *Luther, the analogy of faith was linked to the person of Christ—specifically, all of Scripture should be interpreted as testifying to Christ. For John *Calvin, the principle implied that interpretation must be shaped by the Spirit who inspired the writing of the Scriptures. In all these cases, some parts of the Scriptures are regarded as clearer and more definitive than others and are to be used to interpret those less clear passages. *See also* hermeneutics.

analytic philosophy. The type of *philosophy that has been dominant in England since about 1930 and in North America since World War II. Influential early analytic philosophers included Bertrand *Russell and Ludwig *Wittgenstein. Analytic philosophers have no shared body of philosophical views but are distinguished by a style of philosophizing that emphasizes precise language analysis and the use of logical techniques to analyze arguments. (*See* logical positivism.) Analytic philosophy of religion includes vigorous debates about the existence of God, the problem of *evil, the evidential value of *religious experience and even such specific Christian doctrines as the *Trinity, the *incarnation and the *atonement.

angels. Powerful spiritual creatures who serve as messengers and agents of God. Though angels may take bodily form, many philosophers who believe in their reality think of them as immaterial beings. Many who accept the reality of angels as personal beings also believe in fallen angels, or *demons, who have rebelled against divine authority, with Satan as their leader.

animism. A perspective on the world that sees spiritual powers or forces as residing in and controlling all of the natural world. Thus an animist would recognize not only spirits in animals and humans but also the spirits of trees, rivers and other natural entities.

Anselm, St. (1033-1109). Anselm was an archbishop of Canterbury who is noted for his invention of the *ontological argu-

ment for God's existence (in his *Proslogion*) and his classical
formulation of a doctrine of the *atonement that sees Christ's
sacrifice as providing satisfaction for human *sin (in his *Cur
Deus homo,* or *Why God Became Man*). Anselm was a follower of
*Augustine and continued the tradition of "faith seeking un-
derstanding."

anthropomorphism. The human tendency to see other things as
analogous to ourselves. Thus people sometimes see their pets
in overly anthropomorphic terms. In *philosophy of religion,
the term *anthropomorphism* is often used critically, to refer to
views of God that make God seem too similar to finite human
persons. Ludwig *Feuerbach claimed that all theology is anthropomorphic, since God is essentially a projection of unfulfilled human potential.

antirealism. A philosophical theory that denies the mind-inde-
pendent existence of some type of being or of being in general.
The former type of antirealism may be called regional antirealism; the latter may be called global antirealism. Examples of
regional antirealists would be philosophers who reject the independent reality of numbers, abstract entities in general, and
unobservable theoretical entities in science. Global antirealists,
influenced by Immanuel *Kant, typically argue that humans
cannot know reality as it is in itself, independent of our human
concepts. *See also* idealism; realism.

antithesis. A term often used in popular expositions of G. W. F.
Hegel's dialectical logic, though it was rarely used by *Hegel
himself. Hegel's dialectical logic makes heavy use of triads, in
which the second element of the triad in some way undermines or negates the first element, or "thesis," thereby becoming its "antithesis." This opposition is in turn overcome in the
third element, or "synthesis," which is supposed to capture the
truth that is one-sidedly expressed by each of the first two elements while overcoming their one-sidedness. (*See* dialectic.)
The term is also used in Reformed theology by followers of the
Dutch theologian and statesman Abraham Kuyper to denote
the sharp opposition between patterns of thinking that are

faithful to God and those that are shaped by sinful rebellion.

apologetics. The rational defense of Christian faith. Historically, apologetic arguments of various types have been given: philosophical arguments for the existence of God; arguments that the existence of God is compatible with suffering and evil; historical arguments, such as arguments from *miracles and fulfilled prophecies; and arguments from *religious experience, including mystical experience. (*See* argument from prophecy; evil, problem of; mysticism; theistic arguments.) Some distinguish positive apologetics, which attempts to argue for the truth of Christianity, from negative apologetics, which merely attempts to remove barriers to faith by responding to critical attacks.

Aquinas, St. Thomas (1225-1274). The most famous and influential of the medieval philosopher-theologians. Aquinas is noted for his synthesis of Christian theology with the philosophy of *Aristotle. His general approach is summarized in the memorable dictum that "grace presupposes nature and perfects it." He is most famous for the Five Ways, by which he demonstrated the existence of God as the First Cause of such things as motion and design and as the *necessary being that is the cause of the contingent beings in the natural world. Aquinas's writings contain richly developed thinking on a comprehensive set of theological and philosophical topics, including *ethics and political theory. Though Aquinas believed natural reason can prove that God exists, he did not think reason is competent to know God's essence in this life, and he affirmed that many essential Christian beliefs must be accepted on faith because God has revealed them.

argument from prophecy. A type of apologetic argument that attempts to defend the divinely inspired character of prophets (and ultimately of the Scriptures that record the prophecies) by showing that the prophets foretold events whose occurrence could not have been humanly foreseen. Thus an argument from prophecy is essentially an argument that appeals to *miracles. Sometimes the argument is used in a reverse direction.

The fact that the life of Jesus fulfilled certain Old Testament prophecies, for example, is cited to support the claim that Jesus really is the Messiah. Arguments from prophecy have become less popular in an age characterized by critical biblical scholarship, which in many cases claims that apparently fulfilled prophecies were written after the events prophesied occurred.

Aristotle (384-322 B.C.). One of the most famous philosophers of ancient Greece. Although Aristotle had been a student of *Plato, he rejected Plato's doctrine of transcendent Forms in favor of the claim that universal properties exist immanently in particulars, which he saw as a synthesis of form and matter. Aristotle invented logic as a formal discipline and wrote on a wide range of topics, including *metaphysics, *ethics and much that would today be classified as natural *science, including biology and physics. Aristotle's followers are sometimes called Peripatetics because of his habit of lecturing as he walked on the grounds of the Lyceum, his philosophical school in Athens. *See also* philosophy.

Arminianism. A system of Christian doctrine inspired by the thought of Jacobus Arminius (1560-1609), a Dutch theologian and pastor. Arminius taught that God's election for *salvation was conditional on his *foreknowledge of human free choice. Though he thought of himself as a follower of John *Calvin, his views were rejected by the Reformed Synod of Dordt. The relation between human *free will and divine electing *grace is still hotly debated within many Christian denominations, with those who emphasize free will often labeled Arminians.

aseity. The divine property of being completely independent of everything distinct from God himself. Everything other than God depends on God, but God depends on nothing besides himself.

atheism. The philosophical position that denies the reality of the *God of *theism or other divine beings. *See also* agnosticism; faith.

atonement. Christian doctrine that Christ has in some way solved the problems created by human sinfulness, especially the problem of alienation from God. All Christians affirm the reality of the atonement, but no one theory of atonement has found universal acceptance. The most accepted theories include moral influence theories, satisfaction theories and penal substitution theories. *See also* salvation; sin.

attributes of God. Properties such as *omnipotence (being all-powerful), *omniscience (being all-knowing) and *omnipresence (being present everywhere) that have traditionally been ascribed to *God by theists. Since the twentieth century, some have questioned whether all of the attributes traditionally ascribed to God are coherent. Critical questions have been raised about God's *impassibility, *simplicity and *timelessness, and about the nature of God's *immutability.

Augustine, St. (354-430). A philosopher and theologian and the most famous and influential of the church fathers for the Latin (Western) church. After his conversion, memorably described in his *Confessions,* Augustine became a priest and soon a bishop in Hippo in northern Africa. His most famous writings include *On the Trinity* and *City of God,* in which he described human history as an ongoing struggle between two kingdoms—the city of God and the city of man. Augustine is the preeminent member of the great tradition of Christian Platonism, and his thought had an enormous impact both on the Scholastics of the medieval period and on the Protestant Reformers.

authority. That which merits submission or deference. There are many different kinds of authority, with some of the more important kinds being moral, political and religious authority. Religions based on a *special *revelation, such as Christianity and Islam, stand or fall on the basis of the authority possessed by their revelations. Christians have often disagreed strongly on the locus of authority, with Protestants affirming the authority of the Bible alone (*sola Scriptura)* and Catholics and Orthodox Christians assigning greater weight to the church and its historical *traditions. Debate has also centered around criteria for recognizing a valid authority and the relation between authority and *reason. Thomas *Aquinas argued that, though reason cannot certify the content of an authoritative revelation, it can investigate the credentials of an alleged revelation to be truly from God by evidence such as *miracles.

autonomy. A key concept in the ethical theory of Immanuel *Kant, who held that a genuine moral obligation must be seen as legislated by *reason and thus that a rational moral agent is himself the source of moral obligations. Kant saw an individual who behaves in accordance with morality out of a fear of punishment or desire for a reward as heteronomous, not autonomous. Some contemporary radical theologians have argued that the very existence of a Creator-God to whom human beings are responsible would be a threat to human moral autonomy, and consequently they have proposed that God be understood as a humanly invented symbol or idealization.

Averroës (1126-1198). Islamic philosopher whose commentaries on *Aristotle were influential for Christian and Jewish thinkers in the Middle Ages. Averroës followed Aristotle in holding that *immortality is possessed by an impersonal intellect. Some of his Christian followers were reputed to hold to a doctrine of twofold truth whereby what is true in philosophy could be false theologically, thereby resolving the conflict between the Christian belief in a personal *resurrection and an Aristotelian view in which there is no personal immortality. *See also* Islam; Islamic philosophy.

Avicenna (980-1037). Islamic philosopher and physician who developed a synthesis of the metaphysics of *Aristotle and *Neo-Platonism with Muslim monotheism. Avicenna was the focus of an attack by theologian al-Ghazali in *The Incoherence of the Philosophers,* which is rooted in concerns that an affirmation of the eternality of the world and the necessity of *causation undermines the doctrines of *creation and *providence. Avicenna's works had a major influence on Muslim and Jewish philosophers and, in translation, on Western Christian philosophers as well. *See also* Islam; Islamic philosophy.

B

Barth, Karl (1888-1968). One of the most significant theologians of the twentieth century. Barth's early commentary on *Romans* (1918) is widely credited with undermining liberal Protestant theology and inspiring what is sometimes called *neo-ortho-doxy, or dialectical theology, which emphasized the absolute qualitative difference between God and humans and the essential role of *revelation in coming to know God. A German-speaking Swiss theologian, Barth played a key role in the Confessing Church, which stood up against Adolf Hitler in the Barmen Declaration. His most comprehensive work is the multivolume *Church Dogmatics*.

Beatific Vision. The supremely happy or blessed state in which a person enjoys a direct awareness of God. Many religious philosophers have taken the Beatific Vision to be the supreme good that all humans seek, whether they know it or not, though it is generally held that this state can normally be attained, if at all, only after death.

beauty. Today thought of chiefly as a fundamental type of aesthetic value, exemplified in nature and works of art. Many medievals thought that beauty was one of the transcendental properties (along with goodness and unity) that apply to all of being. A long theological tradition, influenced by *Plato's *Symposium*, holds that God is the source of all beauty and can even be identified with beauty in itself. Among postmedieval thinkers, Jonathan *Edwards put great emphasis on the link between God and beauty.

behaviorism. The attempt to understand human beings in terms of observable behavior. Distinctions can be made between scientific behaviorism, which is a research program in psychology that limits itself to observable environmental stimuli and behavior, and philosophical behaviorism, which attempts to understand mental states reductionistically in terms of outward behavior. A philosophical behaviorist, for example, might identify pain with a tendency to engage in characteristic types of behavior, such as grimacing or crying. Some scientific behaviorists wish to commit themselves only to methodological behaviorism as a necessary rule for science, without denying the existence of inner mental states. Behaviorism is today in decline in both psychology and philosophy with the onslaught of the cognitive revolution, though functionalists still emphasize the role of behavior and stimuli (inputs and outputs) in understanding human beings.

belief. The fundamental positive cognitive attitude that commonly takes a proposition as its object. Most philosophers hold that propositional beliefs can be occurrent, in which case there is conscious assent to a proposition, or nonoccurrent, in which case a person has a disposition to assent to a proposition (such as $2 + 3 = 5$) even though the person is not consciously thinking of that proposition. Theologians distinguish belief *that* something is the case from belief *in* a person or ideal, as when a person believes in God or democracy. The latter seems closer to the biblical concept of *faith. It seems clear, however, that belief in God is not possible without some propositional beliefs as well, since one could hardly believe in God if one did not believe that God existed or believe anything about God's character.

Berkeley, George (1685-1753). One of the great trio of British empiricist philosophers, along with John *Locke and David *Hume. Berkeley, who was an Irish Anglican and became a bishop, is famous for his defense of *idealism, holding that only minds and mental events and properties exist. By rejecting the existence of matter and affirming that "to be is to be perceived," Berkeley hoped to undermine the basis for materialistic *atheism. *See also* empiricism.

Boethius (c. 480-525). An important link between the ancient and medieval worlds, Boethius's translations and commentaries on *Aristotle were almost the sole source of medieval knowledge of that philosopher until the mid-twelfth century. Boethius himself attempted a synthesis of Aristotelian and Platonic views, and he developed a classical conception of God's *eternity as the atemporal, all-at-once possession of an infinite life.

Bonaventure, St. (c. 1217-1274). Franciscan medieval philosopher-theologian who, in contrast to Thomas *Aquinas, argued that we can know by *reason and not merely from *revelation that the world had a beginning. Staunchly *Augustinian in approach, Bonaventure made important contributions to *philosophical theology, to mystical theology and to Franciscan spirituality.

Brunner, Emil (1889-1966). Highly influential Swiss theologian, who (along with Karl *Barth) is credited with being the father of *neo-orthodoxy, or dialectical theology. Brunner and Barth had a famous disagreement over the possibility of *natural theology and natural religious knowledge, with Barth arguing an unqualifiedly negative position and Brunner defending a more nuanced view that does not regard such undertakings as completely without value.

Buber, Martin (1878-1965). Leading religious existentialist and prominent Jewish philosopher. Buber's most famous work, *I and Thou,* makes an important distinction between the I-it relation people enjoy with objects and the kind of dialogical relationship between persons that is sometimes possible. Buber argues that such *I-thou relations provide an analogy with how God, who is the ultimate Thou, can be known.

Buddhism. Religion founded by Siddhartha Gautama, the Buddha, or "enlightened one" (c. 563-483 B.C.). Buddhism puts heavy emphasis on desire as the source of suffering and identifies the achievement of selflessness as the cure for this situation. Selflessness can be achieved through the Eightfold Path, freeing the individual from the wheel of *reincarnation and allowing him or her to achieve nirvana. Buddhism is divided into Theravada Buddhism and Mahayana Buddhism, the latter putting more emphasis on the role of the Buddha himself as a compassionate helper.

Bultmann, Rudolf (1884-1976). German New Testament scholar and theologian who was strongly influenced by the early philosophy of Martin *Heidegger. Bultmann pioneered the use of form criticism, which tries to uncover oral sayings and traditions that underlie the New Testament and understand the development of those traditions in light of the situation of the early church. Bultmann's theology embodies an attempt to "demythologize" the conceptual framework of the New Testament by translating its message using concepts from *existentialism.

burden of proof. Legal term that indicates which party in a controversy has the responsibility of offering support for its position. Thus, in a U.S. criminal trial, the burden of proof rests with the prosecution; the defendant is presumed innocent unless the prosecution can establish guilt. In philosophy, the question of which party has the burden of proof is often disputed. Thus some nonbelievers assert "the presumption of atheism," claiming that if we do not have a proof of God's existence, then *atheism is the rational position. Philosophers in the *Reformed Epistemology camp, on the other hand, argue that belief in God can be perfectly rational even without proof or any arguments at all, so long as there are no sound arguments against God's existence. A middle position holds that neither side has any special burden of proof; the most reasonable view is simply the one that makes the most sense in light of all that is known.

Butler, Joseph (1692-1752). Anglican bishop who made important contributions to both *theology and *philosophy. Butler's *Analogy of Religion* was well known in the eighteenth century for its defense of orthodox Christianity over against *deism. Butler made many acute contributions to moral philosophy, including a celebrated critique of *hedonism, in which he argued that pleasure is not generally the direct object of desire but rather is a byproduct of other things that humans desire.

C

Calvin, John (1509-1564). French Reformation theologian and founder of the tradition that today is most strongly represented in Presbyterian and Reformed churches. Calvin worked out his theological views while attempting to reform the Swiss city of Geneva. (In that tradition Calvinists since have often attempted redemptively to transform the various spheres of human society.) Calvin's thought puts great emphasis on the *sovereignty of God and the ways in which *sin deforms the whole of human existence. Epistemologically, Calvinism puts emphasis on an innate sense of God's reality that has been damaged by sin, on *revelation and on the inner testimony of the Holy Spirit. *See also* Reformed tradition.

Camus, Albert (1913-1960). French existentialist novelist and essayist. Camus is famous for his depiction of the absurd, which he described as the incongruity between the human self that demands meaning and purpose and an indifferent world that offers none. Camus described an existentialist hero who derives some meaning in this meaningless world by an attitude of revolt. This absurd hero clearly understands the futility of the revolt, but he takes up the burden (like Sisyphus, who rolls a rock up a mountain, even though that rock will inevitably roll down again). Thus he refuses "the leap" which Camus attributes to Søren *Kierkegaard. Born in Algeria and active in the Resistance movement during World War II, Camus's life was tragically cut short by an automobile accident. *See also* existentialism.

Cappadocian fathers. A group of theologians most noted for their development of the orthodox doctrine of the *Trinity and their battle with Arianism. Writing between the Council of Nicaea (325) and the Council of Constantinople (381), these church fathers included Basil of Caesarea, Gregory of Nyssa and Gregory of Nazianzus. Their understanding of the Trinity puts relatively more emphasis on the threeness of God than is characteristic of Latin theologians such as *Augustine and inspired a twentieth-century view known as *social trinitarianism.

Carnell, Edward John (1919-1967). One of the leading evangelical theologians and apologists in the twentieth century. Carnell was the first resident president of Fuller Theological
Seminary and was a leader in helping the evangelical movement differentiate itself from *fundamentalism, which he criticized as a form of "cultic Christianity." Carnell's apologetic
arguments tended to link the case for Christianity with our
knowledge of values and ourselves, and he was one of the first
evangelicals to write about Søren *Kierkegaard.

categorical imperative. The supreme principle of *morality,
according to Immanuel *Kant. Kant distinguished between a
hypothetical imperative, which commands an *action condi-
tionally as a means to an end that does not necessarily have
to be willed (such as "Brush your teeth regularly if you want
to avoid having cavities"), and a categorical imperative,
which commands an action absolutely. Kant believed that
there is only one categorical imperative: to act only on the basis of maxims that can be universally willed as a rational law.
He thought that this one imperative could be formulated in
several different ways, including the famous formula of the
end in itself, in which we are enjoined to act in such a manner
that we always recognize that rational agents have intrinsic
worth and dignity and are not to be treated merely as a
means to our own ends.

categories. Constituents of a philosopher's most basic classification scheme. The first philosopher to develop a set of categories was *Aristotle, who famously included ten, namely
substance, relation, quantity, quality, place, time, property,
position, doing and being affected. Another famous categorial
distinction is that which René *Descartes drew between two
fundamental kinds of substance: mental substance and physical substance. Immanuel *Kant is famous for his argument that
the basic categories of the understanding are provided by the
mind and thus that it is impossible for us to know the world as
it is in itself; we know it only as it is structured by our own fun-

damental concepts. His view has inspired a variety of views known collectively as *antirealism.

category mistake. Misunderstanding by regarding a term that belongs to one logical category as if it belonged to a different logical category. Philosopher Gilbert Ryle, who popularized this concept, gave as an example someone who is shown an auditor's report on the financial accounts of a college. This reader of the report confusedly thinks that what is described in the report must be the real college, since the report covers all aspects of the college, and that experiences of the college's buildings, classrooms, libraries and so on must somehow be illusory. Mistakes of this sort are thought by Ryle and others to be grounded in the misunderstanding of language and are regarded as the ground of many philosophical puzzles.

causation. The fundamental kind of relation expressed by such terms as *produce, originate* and *bring about.* The items related (causes and effects) may be persons, objects, states of affairs or events. *Aristotle recognized four types of causality: efficient, final, formal and material. David *Hume famously tried to analyze causality as a constant conjunction between different types of events. Philosophers such as Thomas *Reid have argued for a fundamental type of causation known as "agent causality," in which persons (not merely events occurring in persons) bring about effects. Important philosophical disputes in this area include debates about *determinism (Are all events causally determined, or do persons sometimes possess *free will?) and about the *principle of sufficient reason, which in some forms holds that all events (at least of a certain type) or all contingent substances must have a cause. This principle plays a key role in *cosmological, or first cause, arguments for God's existence.

chain of being. A key element in the worldview of many ancient, medieval and early modern philosophers, who assumed a principle of plenitude in which beings of every possible type must be actualized, from the lowest to the highest. Thus in the medieval world it was common to think of various entities as possessing different degrees of being, from insignificant bare specks of matter through plants and animals and humans and on to angelic beings and God himself, who possesses the highest possible degree of being. The universe is a vast hierarchy of beings, and it is good that all positions in the hierarchy are filled. *See also* Neo-Platonism.

character. The comprehensive set of traits that make up the intellectual and ethical substance of a person. A character is primarily a set of dispositions to behave in certain ways in characteristic circumstances. To evaluate a person's character is to focus on the abiding *virtues, or excellences, in a person over time instead of simply looking at individual *actions.

Chesterton, G. K. (1874-1936). A prolific, imaginative writer in many fields, today best known as a Christian apologist and for his Father Brown detective stories. Some of Chesterton's most-read works include *Orthodoxy, Heretics, The Everlasting Man* and *The Man Who Was Thursday*. He was a major influence on C. S. *Lewis.

Christology. The branch of Christian *theology that attempts to clarify the identity and nature of Jesus of Nazareth, understood as "the Christ" (from the Greek equivalent to the Hebrew term Messiah, which means "anointed one"). Within orthodox Christianity, Christology is concerned with understanding how Jesus can be both divine and human, and with the significance of his life, death and resurrection. *See also* incarnation.

City of God. Classic work (written between 413 and 426) by *Augustine of Hippo, in which human history is interpreted as a struggle between an earthly kingdom founded on self-love and a divinely established society founded on God's *grace.

Clarke, Samuel (1675-1729). English philosopher, theologian and preacher who is closely linked to Isaac Newton's scientific thought. Clarke championed orthodoxy from the viewpoint of *rationalism over against *deism and developed an original and powerful version of the *cosmological argument. He also defended Newton's views of space and time against those of Gottfried *Leibniz.

Clement of Alexandria (c. 150-220). One of the church fathers who, in contrast to *Tertullian, took a positive attitude toward *philosophy and Greek learning. Clement held that the Greek writers were able to discern important truths because the divine wisdom, or *Logos, is present in all humans. Though philosophy is inferior to and cannot substitute for *revelation, Clement thought its study can deepen one's understanding of revelation.

cognition, cognitive. The process by which knowledge is gained, and that which pertains to that process. What is cognitive is knowable, and thus a cognitive proposition is one that can be true or false. *Logical positivism is distinguished by the claim that the only genuine cognitive propositions (other than analytic ones that are made true by linguistic meaning) are those that can be verified by sense experiences. Positivists claim that theological propositions fail this test and thus lack cognitive meaning, though they might have poetic or emotive meaning. *See also* noncognitivism.

coherentism. An epistemological theory holding that the justification for *beliefs consists in the relations among the beliefs. A coherentist thus typically denies that there are any special propositions that are basic or foundational. Rather, the structure of beliefs is like a web in which some beliefs are more central than others but in which some beliefs give mutual support to others as part of a network. More radical forms of coherentism not only adopt a coherentist account of justification but also a coherentist account of *truth, in which true propositions are those that would be part of an ideally coherent system of beliefs. *See also* epistemology.

colonialism, paternalism, imperialism. Critical terms used by multiculturalists for academic work that they see as permeated by attitudes of Western superiority. The criticized views are often associated with male domination as well.

common grace. The *grace of God that is extended not only to the elect whom God saves but to all human creatures and even to the natural order as a whole. Theologians who emphasize common grace say that it is God's gracious action ("sending rain upon the just and the unjust") that makes it possible for sinful humans to acquire knowledge and develop such positive cultural achievements as government and the arts.

Common Sense philosophy. Often referred to as "Scottish Common Sense philosophy" or "Scottish realism," this type of philosophy was originated by Thomas *Reid and was popular both in Great Britain and in North America throughout the nineteenth century. Reid argued against what he took to be the skepticism of David *Hume by trying to show that the principles underlying *skepticism were more dubious than the principles of common sense. While not indubitable, said Reid, the principles of common sense are universally knowable and in practice impossible to reject. Common Sense philosophers like Reid usually defended basic principles of morality and religion as well as the reliability of memory and sense perception and the basic credibility of testimony. *See also* realism.

communitarianism. Form of political philosophy, traceable to G. W. F. *Hegel. Communitarianism rejects the liberal view that takes individual rights to be the foundation of society, putting in its place a view that sees individuals as constituted by the groups of which they are a part. Communitarians are therefore concerned to foster strong communities and social institutions, believing that these social institutions can have rights and obligations in themselves and also that they can create rights and obligations for individuals.

compatibilism. In philosophy of action, the view that causal *determinism is logically compatible with *free will. The compatibilist who accepts both determinism and free will is called a soft determinist. Compatibilism usually defines free will as an *action that is caused by the individual's own desires or wishes, rather than being coerced by some external power. The alternative possibilities that seem necessary for genuine free will are interpreted by compatibilists as hypothetical in character. For example, the individual who freely gave money to a charity could have refrained from giving the money *if* the individual had wished to do so or *if* the situation had been different. Critics of compatibilism argue that genuine freedom requires an individual to have more than one possibility that is actually possible at the time of choosing, not merely possibilities that would be open if certain facts that do not obtain were to obtain.

complementarity. Physicist Niels Bohr's term for his view that that there are alternative, seemingly incompatible descriptions of the world that are nonetheless true or at least necessarily must be accepted. The principle of complementarity is linked to quantum mechanics and the uncertainty principle, which makes it impossible to specify both a specific location and a specific motion for subatomic particles. The classical example of complementarity is the way light must be understood as consisting of both waves and particles. Some theologians and philosophers of science have sought to extend the principle of complementarity metaphorically so as to understand how theological and scientific descriptions of the world could both be true.

conceptualism. Compromise position between *realism and *nominalism on the question of the status of universals such as "goodness." The realist claims that these universals exist objectively, independently of the mind. The nominalist holds that universals are merely names that refer to a group of particulars. The conceptualist holds that real concepts are associated with universal terms but that these concepts do not exist independently of the mind.

Confucianism. Chinese school of ethical, political and religious teachings commonly attributed to Confucius (c. 551-479 B.C.). Confucianism places great weight on the cultivation of ethical virtues such as kingliness, humaneness and gentlemanliness that are cultivated through rituals. Ethical duties within Confucianism depend on one's social and family position. There is some dispute over the religious character of Confucianism, centering on the nature of *tian,* or "heaven," which is in some way the ground of our ethical duties. Some have interpreted this concept in a transcendent, metaphysical way, while neo-Confucians tend to think of "heaven" as a metaphorical way of describing the natural ethical order of things.

conscience. The faculty that approves or disapproves of conduct from a moral point of view. Joseph *Butler made conscience (understood as a divinely implanted faculty) the centerpiece of his moral theory, arguing that, although following conscience does in fact lead to the best consequences for everyone in the long run, the authority of conscience is preeminent and not based on results. In the medieval period many thinkers viewed conscience as the natural human ability to grasp the moral order, but Thomas *Aquinas described that ability as "synderisis" and distinguished it from conscience, which is an ability to apply moral principles to particular situations. *See also* morality.

consciousness. Psychological states such as pain, sensations, thoughts and other objects of mental awareness are called conscious states. There appears to be something deeply private and mysterious about consciousness, leading some philosophers to doubt whether it is possible to truly know the content of others' consciousness (the problem of other minds). Consciousness is a key dimension of the *mind-body problem. Many dualists cite consciousness as the defining property of mental or spiritual reality, and materialists have great difficulty explaining it, leading some (such as advocates of logical *behaviorism and *eliminative materialism) to the extreme position of denying the existence of consciousness altogether. (*See* dualism; materialism.) Contemporary neurological research attempts to understand the physical basis of consciousness. Attempts by cognitive scientists to design a conscious computer implicitly assume philosophical stances toward consciousness.

consequentialism. An ethical theory that sees the ethical goodness or wrongness of an act as determined by the nonmoral consequences of the act, such as the amount of pleasure or pain the act produces. A good example is *utilitarianism, which claims that the morally right act is the one that produces the best consequences for all who will be affected. Consequentialist theories are contrasted with *deontological theories, which hold that rightness and wrongness are not completely determined by consequences.

conservation of creation. Although popular views of *creation understand God's activity to be concerned with the origination of the universe, traditional theological accounts have held that the continued existence of the universe is also essentially linked to God's creative activity. On this view, God's activity in conserving the universe is really the same as his activity in beginning it. *See also* providence.

contingency. A characteristic of finite things that exist but do not exist necessarily. Those who support the *cosmological argument believe that the contingency of the natural order shows that it must have its ground of existence outside itself and that the ultimate ground for the existence of contingent things must be a being whose existence is not contingent but necessary—a being identifiable as God. *See also* necessary being.

conversion. Within Christianity, the change in an individual that represents the beginning of new life in Christ. For many who come to *faith as adults, conversion represents a specific experience. The nature of this conversion experience and its evidential status is debated by psychologists and philosophers of religion. It is noteworthy that conversions to other religions and even secular "faiths" such as Marxism are possible as well. *See also* salvation.

correspondence theory of truth. Most natural and widely held view of propositional *truth, which holds that a proposition is true if it corresponds to or agrees with reality. The core of the correspondence theory of truth is the commonsense notion that the truth or falsity of a proposition is determined by an independent reality. Thus this view of truth is linked to metaphysical *realism. When developed beyond this commonsense notion of truth (for example, by the metaphysical postulation of a realm of facts corresponding to propositions), the correspondence theory becomes controversial. Its major rivals are the coherentist and pragmatic theories of truth, which tie truth closely to human thinking and human acting, respectively. *See also* coherentism; pragmatism.

cosmological arguments. A family of arguments for the existence of God that postulate God's existence as the ultimate cause or ground or explanation of the cosmos. Cosmological arguments normally make use of some principle of explanation, causality or *sufficient reason. Thomas *Aquinas and Samuel *Clarke are among the more famous proponents of this type of argument. *See also* theistic arguments.

counterfactuals. A conditional proposition (usually expressed in the form "if *p*, then *q*") in which the antecedent (*p*) is false. Examples include such propositions as "If the moon were made of green cheese, then it would be tasty" and "If Abraham Lincoln had not been assassinated, then racial reconciliation after the Civil War would have been advanced." There is a vigorous debate over the status of counterfactuals that deal with free human actions, such as "If John had been offered a $5,000 bribe, he would have freely refused it." Advocates of Molinism claim that such propositions have a truth value that God does not determine. (*See* middle knowledge.) They claim as well that God knows all such propositions and uses this knowledge in the providential governance of the universe. This allows God to control the outcome of events without impinging on human freedom. *See also* determinism; free will; providence.

covenant. A mutually binding relationship between two or more parties. A covenantal relationship goes beyond a mere contractual relationship by its formation of genuine bonds between the parties. In theology, *covenant* refers to God's gracious acts in establishing real relations with his human creatures. Theologians in the *Reformed tradition have given special emphasis to the notions of covenant and covenant people in attempting to understand the biblical narrative.

creation. God's activity in originating and maintaining the universe and any other creatures that may exist, such as *angels and *demons. Christian theology holds that God created the world freely out of nothing *(ex nihilo)* and that, although God is immanently present in creation, he transcends that creation.

creation order. Lawlike structure or order that is rooted in God's intentions at *creation. Those who affirm this notion typically think that there are particular "orders" or "spheres" of creation, such as the state and the family, each with its own purposes and norms. The term is also used to refer to a particular order or sphere.

creationism. (1) The theory that God's creation occurred directly and not through some Darwinian mechanism of evolution. Many creationists teach that the universe is relatively young (ten to fifty thousand years old), though some advocates of *intelligent design are willing to entertain the idea of an older universe. (2) The theory that the *soul of each human being is created directly by God and infused into the person, rather than being a biological product of the father and mother.

cultural relativism. *See* relativism.

cumulative case arguments. Arguments for the existence of God (or some other complex claim) that do not consist of a single decisive argument but rather try to show that God's existence makes more sense than any alternative hypothesis in light of all the available evidence. Richard *Swinburne, for example, presented a large number of arguments, none of which has decisive force. But since each argument has some evidential force, the cumulative case is alleged to make the existence of God probable. *See also* theistic arguments.

Cupitt, Don (1934-). Radical English theologian who has explicitly embraced *atheism in books such as *Taking Leave of God.* Cupitt became well known for producing a BBC documentary series, *The Sea of Faith,* which spawned a network of the same name devoted to theological *antirealism, which views religions as human constructions.

D

Daly, Mary (1928-). Feminist theologian who began as a Roman Catholic but moved to a "post-Christian" radical feminist position in *Beyond God the Father*. Daly argues that traditional *theism is a patriarchal, hierarchical view rooted in male-dominated cultures. *See also* feminism; gender; patriarchy, matriarchy.

Daoism. *See* Taoism.

Darwinism. The theory of the development of biological life originated by Charles Darwin (1809-1882), which holds that the mechanism for evolutionary development is made up of chance variations and natural selection involving competition for survival and reproduction. Darwinism sharply reduced the popularity of the argument from *design in England and North America. Many religious thinkers regard Darwinism as compatible with the view that God is the Creator of the universe, seeing natural selection as a means employed by God. Nevertheless, atheists often regard Darwinism as strongly supporting their *worldview. That opinion is shared by many advocates of "creation science," who advocate non-Darwinian accounts of the origin of species. Darwinian thought is influential today in such fields as psychology and sociology. Advocates of Darwinian approaches view many aspects of human culture, even such things as *ethics and religion, with respect to presumed reproductive advantages they provide. *See also* creationism; evolution, theory of.

death, survival of. Continued existence past the end of a person's biological life. All of the great religions in some way give an answer to the question of what happens after death and the implications of this answer for the meaning of life and death. Some of the alternative ways humans have been thought to survive death include *reincarnation, disembodied existence of the *soul and bodily *resurrection, with the latter two being regarded as successive states by many Christians. Options to personal survival include absorption into some absolute mind and being remembered by God. Some contemporary antirealist theologians think of survival after death not as a possible factual state of affairs but as a picture or myth that is intended to give meaning to life here and now. Philosophical questions raised by the possibility of survival of death center on questions of personal *identity and the relation of the person to the body.

deductive argument. A chain of reasoning in which a series of propositions (the premises), if true, are supposed necessarily to imply the truth of another proposition (the conclusion) by virtue of certain logical principles or rules of inference. A deductive argument is logically *valid* when the truth of the premises does in fact necessarily imply the truth of the conclusion, whether or not all of the premises are true. If an argument is logically valid, then all other arguments that have the same logical form will also be valid. A deductive argument is logically *sound* when all of the premises are true and it is logically valid. Classical examples of deductive reasoning are given by the syllogisms of traditional logic, which include such arguments as the following: (1) "All humans are mortal; Socrates is a human; therefore Socrates is mortal." (This example conforms to the argument form "All A is B; p is A; therefore p is B.") (2) "Either George W. Bush is a Democrat or God exists; George W. Bush is not a Democrat; therefore God exists." (This example conforms to the argument form "Either p or q; not p; therefore q.") *See also* inductive reasoning.

deism. The belief that God created the world but is not sustaining it providentially. In other words, though God exists, he has no interaction with the created world. This term is also used to support the view that true religion is a natural religion grounded in *reason rather than any authoritative *special *revelation.

demons. Traditionally viewed as created spiritual beings who have rebelled against God as allies of Satan, their leader. Many liberal theologians regard talk of demons as a symbolic way of speaking about the power of evil. The New Testament records many cases of Jesus or his followers casting out demons from people. Most biblical scholars today accept this material as historical, but those who reject the metaphysical existence of demons explain these possessions as forms of mental illness and regard the stories of exorcism as cases of psychosomatic healing. *See also* angels; evil, nature of.

demythologization. *See* Bultmann, Rudolf.

deontological theory. Ethical theory holding that the rightness or wrongness of *actions is not completely determined by consequences (from Greek *deon, deont-*, meaning "obligation," "necessity"). Thus, a deontologist holds that some actions are wrong in themselves (or at least that they are wrong prima facie), not wrong merely because of the results of the action. Immanuel *Kant is the most famous defender of a deontological ethical theory. Traditional Christian *ethics has also had a deontological strand in holding that some types of actions are absolutely wrong, or wrong in all circumstances.

Derrida, Jacques (1930-). French philosopher who is regarded as the founder of deconstructionism, an important stream in what is often called *postmodernism or poststructuralism. Derrida criticizes modernity for its commitment to "the metaphysics of presence" and what Martin *Heidegger termed "onto-theology." Deconstruction itself fosters a way of thinking that looks for contradictions between the ideals of *modernism and its realities. It also promotes a way of reading that looks for contradictions between what a writer intends to say and what the text actually says. *See also* structuralism.

Descartes, René (1596-1650). French philosopher and mathematician, generally regarded as the father of modern philosophy. Descartes was a rationalist who is well known for his attempt to gain certainty through a process of universal, methodical *doubt in which he posed the possibility that his waking experience was indistinguishable from a dream world as well as the possibility that he was being deceived by an all-powerful evil genius. After establishing clear and distinct ideas as his standard for *truth, Descartes defended soul-body (or mind-body) *dualism and gave a number of proofs for the existence of God.

See also natural light; rationalism; skepticism.

design argument. *See* teleological argument.

design theory. *See* intelligent design.

determinism. The view that all natural events, including human choices and *actions, are the product of past states of affairs in accordance with causal necessity. Thus the determinist holds that, given the state of the universe at any particular time, plus the causal laws that govern events in the natural world, the state of the universe at every future time is fixed. Various kinds of determinism are possible depending on the nature of the causally determining forces. Most determinists today are scientific determinists who believe the laws of nature are the determining factors, but theological determinism, in which God directly determines every event, is also possible. *See also* causation; compatibilism; free will.

Dewey, John (1859-1952). One of the leaders of American *pragmatism and an advocate of democratic liberalism and educational reform. Dewey was committed to philosophical *naturalism and, unlike his fellow pragmatist William *James, had little interest in *religious experience or the possibility of an *afterlife. In *A Common Faith* he attempted to develop a version of religious *faith (or perhaps a successor to such faith) that involved the veneration of the natural order, human potential and the ideals of democracy.

dialectic. A process of thinking or argument that involves contradictions and their resolution, sometimes in the form of questions and opposing answers. The term has been used very differently by different philosophers. *Plato thought of dialectic as the highest form of reasoning. *Aristotle and later medieval philosophers tended to think of dialectic as a formal method of disputation. Immanuel *Kant developed a "transcendental dialectic" that attempted to reveal the contradictions into which uncritical reason falls. G. W. F. *Hegel developed a dialectical logic, which he saw as providing the formal structure of history as well, seen as the progressive unfolding of the Absolute. This historical dialectic was taken over by Karl *Marx and put to use in his dialectical materialism.

dialectical materialism. *See* Marxism.

dialectical theology. *See* neo-orthodoxy.

divine action. Events brought about by God understood as an intentional agent. It is characteristic both of the biblical narrative and of classical theism to see God as a being who acts. Traditional theologians have distinguished between God's actions in creating and conserving the world and its general providential ordering and God's actions in special or particular *providence and *miracles at particular points in history. Some contemporary theologians do not think of God as an intentional agent and so regard all talk of divine action as metaphorical. Others are willing to accept God's activity in *creation but regard "special acts" as events that are brought about through the normal natural order yet have a special revelatory function. Philosophical debates continue about the implications of divine action for God's relation to time and space. *See also* actions (divine and human).

divine attributes. *See* attributes of God.

divine command theories. Ethical theories holding that at least one of the reasons that *actions are right or wrong is that they are commanded or forbidden by God. Philosophers have tended to reject divine command theories, either by alleging that they make ethical duties arbitrary or by claiming that they are incompatible with moral *autonomy. (*See* Euthyphro dilemma.) However, such philosophers as Robert Adams and Philip Quinn have mounted convincing defenses of divine command theories against these criticisms. *See also* ethics.

dogma. A doctrine or teaching of the church. Roman Catholic and Orthodox theologians regard dogmas as those central doctrines formally accepted by the church and not simply asserted by theologians.

Dooyeweerd, Herman (1894-1977). Dutch philosopher and legal scholar whose philosophical thinking was inspired by the Dutch Reformed theologian Abraham Kuyper. Dooyeweerd's philosophy, developed in cooperation with his colleague Dirk

Vollenhoven, is often called "the philosophy of the law-idea." Dooyeweerd viewed philosophies as perspectival—that is, as shaped by fundamental religious attitudes of the heart—and tried to construct a philosophy that is distinctively Christian in that it recognizes the *sovereignty of God in the various spheres of the *creation order.

double effect, principle of. The view that there is a significant moral difference between consequences of an *action that are intended and those that may only be foreseen but not intended. According to this view, for example, it might be morally permissible to administer a pain-relieving drug to a dying person with the intent of alleviating suffering even if it is foreseen that the drug might shorten the life of the dying person. *See also* ethics.

doubt. An attitude of uncertainty, directed toward a proposition or person. As the etymological connection with *double* makes clear, to be in doubt is to be of two minds, unsure of what to believe. René *Descartes proposed adopting universal doubt as the proper method to obtain certainty in philosophy. Thinkers as diverse as Thomas *Reid, David *Hume and Søren *Kierkegaard, on the other hand, have agreed that universal doubt is impossible (and would be incurable if it *were* possible). Though doubt is properly seen as opposed to *faith or *belief, it seems possible for a healthy, living faith (understood as trust) to coexist with some kinds of doubt, as in "I believe; help my unbelief" (Mk 9:24).

dualism. Any philosophical theory that posits two distinct primary substances or that is built around a fundamental distinction between two elements. The term is used in a variety of contexts to designate entirely different kinds of theories. For example, ancient *Manichaeism was a form of dualism postulating two equal but opposing divine realities, a good power of light and an evil power of darkness. *Theism has a dualistic dimension in that it makes a clear distinction between God and the created order, between the infinite and the finite. Theories positing that the mind (or soul) and the body are distinct substances are also referred to as dualisms, though there are important differences among Platonic, Thomistic and Cartesian forms of mind-body dualism.

Duns Scotus, John (c. 1265-1308). Scottish philosopher and theologian, one of the leading figures of *Scholasticism. Scotus was a Franciscan who lectured at Oxford, Paris and Cologne. Called "the subtle doctor," Scotus synthesized the insights of *Augustine with the newer thought in the tradition of *Aristotle. He is well known for his conviction that God created individual essences, or "haecceities," and for his defense of the role of *divine commands or decrees as part of the foundation of *ethics. He taught that the human will has two natural motives: an "affection for advantage" and an "affection for justice."

Durkheim, Émile (1858-1917). French social scientist, one of the founders of modern empirical sociology and pioneer of the sociology of religion. Durkheim developed a naturalistic and functionalist approach to religion (and the rest of society) that sees religious beliefs and rituals as providing a set of unifying symbols that represent the core values of a society. One criticism often made of Durkheim's theory of religion is that it does not seem to capture the universal aspects of the great world religions, which seem to transcend the values of any particular society.

E

ecofeminism. View that lack of concern for the environment is grounded in patriarchal attitudes, including religious constructs that divorce human beings from nature and regard nature as property to be used and managed. *See also* ecological crisis; feminism; gender; patriarchy, matriarchy.

ecological crisis. Emergency precipitated by modern industrial societies, which appear to steadily diminish fresh air, water and unspoiled natural habitats for plants and animals. Historian Lynn White has argued that the ecological crisis is rooted in theistic religions that are anthropocentric and view humans as rulers and managers of the natural order. As a response, some theologians have moved toward *pantheism, *panentheism and *animism, which allegedly view nature as more sacred than does *theism. Theists have responded that the idea of human stewardship does not logically imply that the environment can be spoiled but rather that people ought to care for God's creation.

Edwards, Jonathan (1703-1758). American philosopher and theologian who synthesized *Enlightenment scientific and philosophical ideas with historic Calvinism. Edwards's thought is distinguished by commitments to George *Berkeley's idealism, to *compatibilism with respect to freedom and determinism, and to an interesting view of God's holiness as "the disinterested love of being" that constitutes "true beauty." Edwards believed that a person must have a love for *beauty in this form in order to acquire religious *truth, and thus he devoted much attention to the development of religious affections, or emotions. Edwards is also important as one of the founders of revivalism in North America.

egoism. The theory that humans do or should seek only their own individual *happiness. Psychological egoism holds that as a matter of fact people seek always and only their own good. Moral egoism holds that it is right or good that humans should act in this way. Ayn Rand's novels provide a dramatic illustration and defense of egoism. Traditional Christian teaching, in contrast, has condemned universal egoism as a form of sinful selfishness, to be distinguished from a proper regard for one's *self and its needs. *See also* hedonism.

eliminative materialism. Form of *materialism that denies the existence of distinctively mental entities rather than seeing mental states as identical with or reducible to physical states. Thus an eliminative materialist might argue that in principle an ideal scientific account of the world would contain no reference to such mental entities as "beliefs" or "sensations." The eliminative materialist, instead of arguing that entities such as "pains" are really just brain processes of a certain sort, claims that when science progresses we will be able to say that talk of what we used to call (confusedly and mistakenly) "pains" has been replaced by talk of appropriate types of brain processes.

embodiment. A central theme of European *phenomenology that focuses on the body not merely as a physiological object but as *my* body—the body as experienced or lived. The term is also used by panentheists who reject the traditional theistic view of God as transcending the world and instead think of God as embodied in the natural order. *See also* panentheism.

empiricism. Type of epistemological theory that, in contrast with epistemological *rationalism, gives primacy to sense experience in the acquisition of *knowledge. There are many types of empiricism. In the ancient world, *Aristotle was much more empiricist than was *Plato, who emphasized innate ideas. This same difference was reflected in medieval philosophers, some of whom were Platonists, while others, such as Thomas *Aquinas, followed Aristotle more closely. In modern philosophy the British philosophers John *Locke, George *Berkeley and David *Hume are the most significant empiricists. In the twentieth century *logical positivism and its successors represented the empiricist tradition. *See also* epistemology.

Enlightenment. Eighteenth-century intellectual movement that emphasized the *autonomy of human *reason and questioned the role of traditional *authorities. Immanuel *Kant and David *Hume were among the most important thinkers of the Enlightenment, though it included such individuals as Thomas Jefferson as well. Kant's motto "Dare to use your own reason" expresses the attitude of the Enlightenment well. Kant and Hume both developed influential critiques of the rational grounds of religious belief, though Kant himself thought that in denying religious *knowledge he was making room for rational religious *faith.

epistemology. The branch of *philosophy concerned with questions about *knowledge and *belief and related issues such as *justification and *truth. Some conceive of epistemology as an attempt to refute *skepticism, the denial that knowledge is possible. One of the major debates in epistemology is that of internalism versus externalism: Must the basis or ground that warrants a belief be internally accessible to *consciousness? Another major debate is *foundationalism versus *coherentism: Are some beliefs "properly basic," or are all beliefs based on other beliefs in an interconnected web? Some philosophers of religion have argued that critiques of religious belief as unreasonable are grounded in faulty epistemologies, theories of knowledge that if applied to fields other than religion would make knowledge impossible in those other fields as well.

equivocal. Adjective that describes the status of a term when it is used in more than one sense in the course of an argument, so that the argument commits the logical fallacy of equivocation. Note the equivocal use of terms in the following humorous example: "I love you. Therefore I am a lover. All the world loves a lover. You are all the world to me. Therefore you love me."

eschatological verification. View that the truth or falsity of religious statements is capable of empirical verification—but only after death. John *Hick developed this view as a response to the logical positivist charge that religious propositions are cognitively meaningless because they are not empirically verifiable. *See also* empiricism; logical positivism; language, religious (theories of).

eschatology. Branch of *theology that deals with the "last things," or the end of history, including such topics as the second coming of Christ, the final *judgment and the nature of *heaven and *hell.

essentialism. Metaphysical view that there are real essences, or "natures," in things. Objects have sets of properties that are essential to their being what they are, and these can be distinguished from those properties they have "accidentally" or contingently. An opposing view holds that essences are a function of language. According to this opposing view, the set of properties essential to an object is a function of how the object is being described rather than a real feature of the object. *See also* metaphysics.

eternity/everlasting. Contrasting ways of thinking of God's relation to *time as well as the nature of the life hoped for by Christians now and after death. There is a dispute between those who think of eternity as everlasting time, with no beginning or end, and those who conceive of eternity as an atemporal (timeless) mode of reality. Defenders of the notion of eternity as everlasting argue that this is the Hebraic concept and that the concept of a timeless eternity is a product of Greek thinking that distorts the biblical view. Defenders of timeless eternity argue that God is the Lord of time and that he could not create time without himself being timeless.

ethics. Branch of *philosophy that concerns itself with questions of right and wrong, *good and *evil, *virtues and vices. In addition, ethics deals with metaethical questions, such as "What does it mean to call an act 'right'?" "What is the basis or foundation of rightness?" "What makes right acts right?" The dispute concerning consequentialist and *deontological ethical theories is one of the major areas of disagreement in ethics.

Euthyphro dilemma. Dilemma inspired by an argument in *Plato's *Euthyphro* dialogue that is alleged to undermine *divine command theories in ethics. The key question is whether acts are right because God commands them or whether God commands certain acts because they are right. If one chooses the first option, it is alleged that moral rightness will be based on an arbitrary decision on God's part and that it will then be meaningless to praise God as righteous. If one chooses the second horn of the dilemma, then it appears that what is right must be independent of God's commands.

evidentialism. The view that religious beliefs (as well as other kinds) are only *rational if they are based on evidence. Typically, evidentialists will specify some minimum of evidence that is sufficient (such as "evidence that makes a belief more probable than not" or "evidence that makes a belief more probable than its competitors"). Another popular form of evidentialism is a proportional "ethics of belief" that holds that the strength of one's assent to a *belief should be proportioned to the strength of the evidence. This kind of ethic of belief can be traced to John *Locke. Evidentialism has been strongly challenged by *Reformed Epistemology, particularly the work of Alvin *Plantinga and Nicholas *Wolterstorff.

evil, nature of. The character of that which is opposed to *good. Christians think of evil as what is opposed to the purposes of God. Most Christian theologians have held that evil is not a positive thing or substance but should be understood as a defect or damage to God's creation. Though evil is not a substance, it does have a positive, active character in that it is rooted in the actions of free agents. The question of its character is therefore closely linked to questions about the nature of personal freedom and the relations between such creatures and their Creator.

evil, problem of. Difficulty posed by the existence of *evil (both moral evil and natural evil) in a world created by a God who is both completely good and all-powerful. Some atheists argue that if such a God existed, there would be no evil, since God would both want to eliminate evil and would be able to do so. An argument that evil is logically incompatible with God's reality forms the logical or deductive form of the problem. An argument that evil makes God's existence unlikely or less likely is called the evidential or probabilistic form of the problem. Responses to the problem include theodicies, which attempt to explain why God allows evil, usually by specifying some greater good that evil makes possible, and defenses, which argue that it is reasonable to believe that God is justified in allowing evil, even if we do not know what his reasons are. *See also* free will defense; theodicy.

evolution, theory of. Theory that life forms have altered or evolved over time. Microevolution is development within a species and is uncontroversial. Macroevolution is the theory that various life forms have evolved from simpler life forms, often coupled with a theory of common descent that claims all forms of biological life have evolved from one simple organism. Though various evolutionary theories have been developed, the most common theories today are neo-Darwinian. *See also* creationism; Darwinism.

exclusivism. Within Christian *theology, the view that *salvation is possible (at least for adults since the time of Christ) only for those who explicitly have faith in Jesus. This view is contrasted with inclusivism, which holds that, though people can only be saved through Christ, it is possible that some who lack explicit faith in Christ in this life will be saved by him, and pluralism, which holds that Jesus is not the only means of salvation. More broadly, the term is used for any religious view that holds that salvation is possible only through that particular religion.

existentialism. Cluster of philosophies popular after World War II that stressed that human existence is constituted by the choices people make. Existentialists had no agreed-upon body of beliefs but tended to stress the freedom, precariousness and even absurdity of the human situation, along with the responsibility of the individual to define herself or himself through action. Though existentialism was inspired by nineteenth-century thinkers Søren *Kierkegaard and Friedrich *Nietzsche, neither of these philosophers would have endorsed much of what passed as existentialism. There were both atheistic (Jean Paul *Sartre and Albert *Camus) and religious (Martin *Buber and Gabriel-Honoré *Marcel) versions, but in the popular mind existentialism is seen as atheistic.

experience of God. *See* religious experience.

F

faith. Within Christianity, that attitude of trust in God, including beliefs about God and his goodness, that is essential to a right relationship with God. Many theologians regard faith as including various dimensions, including trust, propositional *belief and a willingness to act obediently. More loosely, the term is used for any set of religious commitments or even secular commitments, as with the person who has "faith" in psychoanalysis or Marxism. Also used as a synonym for *religion*, as in "the world's major faiths."

Fall, the. For traditional Christians, the disobedience of Adam and Eve, the parents of the human race, which plunged humanity into *sin and death and led to the marring of God's originally good creation. Many contemporary theologians view the story of the Fall as a myth, considering the narrative to be a pictorial description of the human condition rather than a description of a historical event.

fatalism. The view that whatever happens does so necessarily and that therefore human choice and effort make no difference. Critics of *determinism allege that fatalism is a logical consequence of determinism, but most determinists (particularly so-called "soft determinists") reject this on the grounds that human choices do make a difference as part of the causal order. Some "hard determinists" accept the idea that whatever happens does so necessarily and claim that recognizing this truth frees a person from anxiety and leads to peace of mind.

feminism. Way of thinking that makes the differential experiences of men and women fundamental to its conclusions and methods. Feminists argue that much traditional scholarship in many fields reflects an unconscious male bias, adding that when theorizing takes account of women's interests and identities, it can help overcome these problems. It is important to distinguish among various forms of feminism, such as liberal feminism, socialist feminism and so-called radical feminism. Though many feminists are stridently anti-Christian and even antireligious, some feminists are committed Christians who argue that a concern for women's well-being is grounded in Christian views of equality. *See also* gender; patriarchy, matriarchy.

Feuerbach, Ludwig (1804-1872). German philosopher who developed the projection theory of religion in which God is understood as a projection of unfulfilled human potential. Thus, according to this theory, religion is really anthropology. Feuerbach was a materialist who had a strong influence on Karl *Marx. Feuerbach held that human progress demands a demystification of the religious consciousness and a return to concrete problems of human existence.

fideism. The view that *faith takes precedence over *reason. The word is often used as a term of abuse to designate a view considered by a critic to be a form of irrationalism. *Tertullian and Søren *Kierkegaard are often cited as fideists.

finitude. Those limitations in the natural order that are to be ascribed to creatureliness rather than to *sin. Thus sin itself must be understood not merely as a defect due to finitude but to a willful turning away from God. Being finite with respect to moral insight or will does not constitute sin; willful failure to follow a moral insight, however, cannot merely be ascribed to finitude.

first cause. *See* cosmological arguments.

Five Ways. *See* Aquinas, Thomas.

foreknowledge, divine. God's knowledge of future events, including future free human choices. Some philosophers argue that since God's knowledge cannot be mistaken, and since the past cannot be changed, God's knowing future events before they occur implies that no other events could possibly occur and that *free will is an illusion (the *determinism viewpoint). A variety of responses to this problem have been given, including holding that since God is timeless he has no knowledge *before* an event but knows all things in a timeless now. Others accept Molinism, the view that God's foreknowledge and *providence are linked to his *middle knowledge, which is a knowledge of how free creatures would act in different circumstances. Still others limit God's foreknowledge by holding that, while *omniscience includes knowing all true or false propositions, some propositions about the future are as of yet neither true nor false. And similarly, others limit divine foreknowledge by holding that, while God knows all that it is logically possible to know, it is logically impossible to have infallible prior knowledge of free decisions.

foundationalism. Type of *epistemology holding that though many *beliefs are based on other beliefs, some beliefs must be held in a basic or foundational manner in order to avoid an infinite regress of beliefs. Classical foundationalism held that basic beliefs must be highly certain (self-evident or experientially certain) to be properly held, while some contemporary foundationalists, such as advocates of *Reformed Epistemology, accept the fallibility of basic beliefs. *See also* foundationalism, classical.

foundationalism, classical. Type of *epistemology that was predominant in early modern philosophy through the *Enlightenment. As a version of foundationalism, this type of epistemology holds that *beliefs must be grounded on basic or foundational beliefs. However, classical foundationalism is distinguished from such fallibilist epistemologies as *Reformed Epistemology by the claim that foundational beliefs must be highly certain. Rationalist versions held that the foundational beliefs must be self-evidently true, while empiricists accepted propositions that are "incorrigible" because they are evident to the senses as possessing the requisite degree of certainty. Many philosophers today are convinced that the ideal of classical foundationalism cannot be attained and that as a consequence we must either become *skeptics or else embrace some alternative epistemology, such as a nonfoundationalist *coherentism or a fallibilist version of foundationalism.

free will. The ability of an agent to make genuine choices that stem from the *self. Libertarians argue that free will includes the power to determine the will itself, so that a person with free will can will more than one thing. Compatibilists typically view free will as the power to act in accordance with one's own will rather than being constrained by some external cause, allowing that the will itself may ultimately be causally determined by something beyond the self. Hard determinists deny the existence of free will altogether. Most Christian theologians agree that humans possess free will in some sense but

disagree about what kind of freedom is necessary. The possession of free will does not entail an ability not to *sin, since human freedom is shaped and limited by human *character. Thus
a human person may be free to choose among possibilities in
some situations but still be unable to avoid all sin. *See also* compatibilism; determinism; libertarianism (metaphysical).

free will defense. Response to the problem of *evil arguing that
God may be justified in allowing evil because the possibility of
evil is logically inherent in *free will. If free will is a great
*good that makes possible other great goods, then these goods
might provide a sufficient reason for God allowing evil. Since
not even omnipotence can do what is logically impossible,
God must accept the possibility of evil if he wishes to give
some of his creatures free will. *See also* theodicy.

Freud, Sigmund (1856-1939). Austrian physician and psychological theorizer, founder of psychoanalysis. In *philosophy of
religion, Freud is known for his theory that belief in God is an
illusion that arises out of the Oedipal complex, in which a child
has a relation to what appears to the child to be an all-powerful
father, on whom the child is dependent and whose good will
the child desires. Freud does not appear to have noticed that
his psychological theory, which holds that the child also re-
sents and envies the powerful father, could provide an equally
reductionistic explanation of antireligious beliefs. Nor did he
consider the possibility that the child's relation to the parents,
rather than being a mechanism for the formation of an illusion,
could be a divinely ordained model whereby God provides a
conception of himself.

functionalism. The view that mental states are not defined by
their intrinsic qualities but by their relations to other states,
particularly causal relations. A functionalist would not thereby define a mental state dualistically as a spiritual event nor
materialistically as a brain process but would rather say that a
mental state is simply a state that plays a certain functional role
in an organism's life. Mental states are those that are caused by
certain inputs from the environment, which in turn cause cer-

tain behaviors, and that also enjoy certain relations with other inner states. (The latter type of relation is one factor that distinguishes functionalism from *behaviorism.) In theory a functionalist could be a dualist, but in reality most functionalists about the human mind are physicalists who believe that material states satisfy the functional roles. *See also* dualism.

fundamentalism. Originally a term that designated the movement associated with a group of books written by distinguished theologians in the early part of the twentieth century defending the fundamentals of the Christian faith, especially the deity of Christ. Over time the term has taken on a broader sense, becoming associated with any form of traditional, conservative Christianity and even with traditional and conservative forms of other religions, as in "Muslim fundamentalists." When used in this broader way, the term is often employed in a derogatory manner, with connotations of anti-intellectualism. As a result, conservative Christians often prefer to distinguish their own views from those of fundamentalism, such as by asserting, "I am an evangelical [or 'traditional Christian' or 'neoevangelical'], not a fundamentalist."

G

Gadamer, Hans-Georg (1900-). German philosopher who developed a philosophical hermeneutic that sees interpretation as a fundamental dimension to human existence. Gadamer, who was a student of Martin *Heidegger, criticizes the *Enlightenment for its "prejudice against prejudices" and argues that understanding requires us to grasp a text against a "horizon of meaning" provided by a tradition. The interpreter brings to the encounter his or her own horizon of meaning, and genuine understanding occurs when there is a "fusion of horizons."

Galileo Galilei (1564-1642). Italian astronomer and physicist and one of the great early modern scientists. Galileo invented the modern science of mechanics and defended Copernicus's theory that the sun is the center of the solar system. He was called before the Inquisition and forced to recant his views. This episode is often cited as evidence of the conflict between religion and *science. However, it is noteworthy that Galileo was himself deeply religious and even gave theological justifications for his approach to science.

gender. Originally a term for the grammatical structure of many languages, in which nouns are designated either as masculine or feminine (or neuter, in some languages). Feminist theorists have seized on the word as a term for the way in which sexual differences can be understood not as a biological necessity but as a cultural construction. Thus feminists argue that much traditional scholarship, including theology and philosophy, has reflected a masculine, gender-biased viewpoint that has not taken adequate account of women's experiences and interests. *See also* feminism; patriarchy, matriarchy.

general revelation. Term used for the knowledge about God that he makes possible through the natural world, including general religious experiences of awe and dependence. Defenders of general revelation have usually claimed that it is sufficient only to give us knowledge of the existence of a powerful Creator, though some have argued that the goodness of God can also be seen in the natural order. General revelation is distinguished from the *special revelation God has provided on particular occasions in history through prophets, apostles and supremely (for Christians) Jesus of Nazareth. Special revelation provides more concrete knowledge of the character and actions of God in relation to his creation. *See also* revelation.

Gnosticism. A religious movement popular in the second and third centuries of the Christian church. Gnosticism's influence can be seen in various Christian heresies and in Christian polemics against the movement's tendencies. Gnostics believed in the possibility of a higher level of spiritual *knowledge, or *gnosis*, and recommended various means of achieving this higher spiritual state. Gnostics tended to depreciate the material world in favor of the higher spiritual world. The term is often used more loosely to refer to religious movements of any time period that emphasize esoteric spiritual knowledge.

God. Divine being or beings who are the object of religious *worship or awe. Theists conceive of God as one being who created all things other than himself and who possesses a supremely good set of attributes, such as *omnipotence, *omnipresence and *omniscience, though Christian theists affirm that this one God exists in three persons. Polytheists believe there are multiple divine beings who have supernatural powers but lack the perfections of the God of *theism. Pantheists view God as identical with the natural universe, while panentheists typically see God's relation to the natural world as one of *embodiment. *See also* attributes of God; divine attributes; pantheism; panentheism; polytheism; theism.

God-of-the-gaps argument. A type of argument that invokes God as an explanation for what cannot be explained naturally or scientifically. Critics of this style of argument claim that such a strategy will inevitably make God's role in the universe appear to diminish as scientific explanation advances. Critics of the *intelligent design movement allege that the attempt to argue for an intelligent cause of biological order is a God-of-the-gaps argument, but proponents of intelligent design argue that there is positive empirical evidence for intelligence as the cause of complex systems in nature.

good, the. The most general term of ethical approval. The good is that which has positive value—for humans, that which is constitutive of, or conducive to, human flourishing. "Good" has both a moral sense, in which it is the opposite of *evil, and a nonmoral sense, in which it is the opposite of that which is bad in any sense. Many ethical theories are grounded in a theory of the good, an example being that of the hedonist who identifies the good with pleasure. Theists typically hold that the good is in some way linked to God, who is supremely good. For Platonists, the Good is the supreme Form, the One from whom all being and value is derived, and Christian Platonists have naturally identified the Good with God. *See also* ethics; morality; Platonism.

grace. Traditionally understood by Christians as the unmerited favor of God extended toward his creation and particularly toward humans. Christians think of God's grace as preeminently extended to humans in Jesus' incarnation, death and resurrection, by which God atones for sin and makes possible eternal life with himself. *See also* common grace.

H

happiness. The intrinsically good state of life regarded as supremely worth having. The ancient Greeks tended to agree that happiness, or *eudaimonia*, is the end or goal of the ethical life, while disagreeing about the nature of happiness and how to achieve it. Broadly speaking, *Aristotle tended to think of happiness as consisting mainly of activities. In other words, the happy person is the one who flourishes by actualizing his or her human potential. Hedonists think of happiness more as a life of pleasant experiences. Christians tend to link true happiness with the blessedness found in knowing God. *See also* Beatific Vision; hedonism.

heaven. In Christian *theology, the final state of those who know God and are blissfully united to him in Christ. Though there are many images of heaven employed in Scripture, most theologians agree that humans are at present incapable of understanding the nature of heavenly existence. *See also* hell.

hedonism. The ethical theory that identifies the *good with *happiness and understands happiness as the presence of pleasure and the absence of *pain. Critics of hedonism argue that the hedonist confuses what is a byproduct and concomitant of the good with the good itself; we do not seek pleasure primarily, but we seek good things (love and friendship, for example) that give us pleasure. If we did not value those things intrinsically, they would not in fact give us pleasure at all. *See also* egoism.

Hegel, Georg Wilhelm Friedrich (1770-1831). German philosopher who developed a philosophical system called Absolute Idealism. In this system the whole of reality is seen as the progressive unfolding of an Absolute Mind (identified with God), achieved through a dialectical process in which *Geist* (Spirit or Mind) repeatedly becomes alienated from itself and then overcomes that negation in a higher unity. Hegel saw human history as the place where the Absolute becomes self-conscious, and he saw the modern liberal state as the highest form of Spirit, an ethical community in which art, religion and philosophy—the three forms of Absolute Spirit—can flourish. Both Karl *Marx and Søren *Kierkegaard reacted critically against Hegel while at the same time being influenced by him in many ways.

Heidegger, Martin (1889-1976). German philosopher whose life's work centered on the question of the meaning of being. After early training in theology, Heidegger switched to philosophy to study with phenomenologist Edmund *Husserl. His famous early work *Being and Time* attempted to discern the meaning of being by looking at human being *(dasein)*—that being whose very being involves the question of being and who must resolutely face up to the temporality implied by a person's own death. In his later writings, Heidegger changed his focus toward a mode of philosophizing in which the "call of Being" that has been repressed by technology and instrumental thinking can perhaps be discerned in the poet and the work of art. Heidegger had a great influence on *existentialism, though he repudiated the uses the existentialists made of his work. His embrace of National Socialism has made him a controversial figure, though he remains influential, especially for *postmodern philosophers.

hell. The final state of the damned, those who are separated from God. Many philosophical controversies center around hell, notably the questions posed for *theodicy by the existence of hell. While hell has traditionally been conceived of as a place of unending, conscious torment, some hold that those who are truly separated from God are annihilated, since to be cut off from God completely is to escape being. Thinkers such as C. S. *Lewis have suggested that hell is primarily a consequence of choice rather than a retributive punishment. The final mercy of God's love allows those for whom God's presence would be sheer torment to escape from that presence, though this is a fate that is horrible beyond description for those who understand the good that is thereby lost. *See also* heaven.

henotheism. A religious perspective that ascribes supremacy, or at least supreme loyalty, to one deity (or "high god") while recognizing the existence of other gods. *See also* polytheism.

hermeneutics. Traditionally the subdiscipline of *theology concerned with the proper interpretation of scriptural texts. In the nineteenth and twentieth centuries, the term widened to include the discipline that seeks to understand the interpretation of texts in general, including the proper roles and relationships among author, reader and text. Still more broadly, the term has been used by philosophers such as Hans-Georg *Gadamer and Paul *Ricoeur to refer to the attempt to articulate the nature of understanding itself, with an emphasis on the role of interpretation as a key component in all human knowing. Here the interpretation of texts, with the taken-for-granted horizons of meaning that reading presupposes, becomes a metaphor for human understanding in general, and such things as human lives themselves are seen as "texts" or text analogues.

Hick, John (1922-). Influential philosopher of religion, whose views have shifted toward a pluralistic view of the world's religions. Earlier in his career Hick defended the *cognitive meaningfulness of religious *language over against *logical positivism and developed an influential "soul-making" *theodicy. More recently, Hick has argued that each of the world's religions represents a culturally conditioned response to "the Real" and that one cannot pragmatically judge one religion as superior to others. In Christian theology Hick has argued that the *incarnation of Jesus cannot be literally true. *See also* religious pluralism.

Hildegard of Bingen (1098-1179). Theologian, musician and artist of the medieval period whose thought and music are receiving renewed attention. Hildegard's life and writings were marked by great originality and a deep *mysticism.

Hinduism. The dominant religious perspective of India, which is defined by the *authority of the religious writings called the Vedas and the Upanishads. Hinduism is more a group of religious traditions than a single religious faith, since within Hinduism one can find both theistic and monistic views of God and profound disagreements about such things as the nature of *personal identity. Generally, Hinduism is characterized by an acceptance of the doctrine of *reincarnation, or transmigration of the soul, and the goal of the religious devotee is seen as the deliverance of the soul from the cycle of reincarnation. *See also* monism; theism.

historical Jesus. The reconstructed portrait that is the goal of historical study dealing with Jesus of Nazareth. Beginning in the late eighteenth century and continuing through the present, with some starts and stops, there has proceeded a movement called the quest for the historical Jesus, an attempt to recover by objective historical inquiry the so-called Jesus of history, who is presumed to have been distorted by church dogma. The "historical Jesus" is sometimes contrasted with the theologically interpreted "Christ of faith," but the church has always affirmed the historicity of the Christ it worships, and it thus has good reasons to welcome genuine historical study. It is, however, unlikely that any historical portrait will not in some ways reflect the "faith" of the historian constructing the portrait.

Hobbes, Thomas (1588-1679). English philosopher best known for his political thought, though he also developed a mechanistic, deterministic, materialistic metaphysic and an empiricist epistemology. In his *Leviathan* Hobbes developed a form of social contract theory, in which humans give up the rights they have in the state of nature, where life is "solitary, poor, nasty, brutish and short," and create a commonwealth by assigning those rights to a sovereign. The sovereign determines what is just and unjust, and thus the sovereign itself (a person or group) cannot be unjust. *See also* empiricism; epistemology; materialism.

holiness. That quality of God and of things and persons set apart for God that marks whatever possesses it as "different" and "other" than the ordinary things of creation. Thus, when Moses met God at the burning bush, he was afraid and was told to remove his sandals, because the place was holy. In the New Testament, holiness increasingly took on the characteristics of righteousness and moral purity. The Holiness Movement is made up of those churches, especially in the Wesleyan tradition, that put a special emphasis on sanctification as a distinct work of *grace. *See also* morality.

holism. A term used in *epistemology for theories of meaning and justification that emphasize systemic interconnections. Theories that view meaning as determined by the relations that concepts have to each other, rather than by the referential relation of language to extralinguistic reality, are often called holistic. Coherentist, nonfoundationalist accounts of justification are also referred to as holistic. (*See* coherentism; foundationalism.) In both cases the image of a web is often used, with meaning or justification said to be a function of the place occupied in the web of concepts or web of beliefs.

hope. One of the primary Christian *virtues, along with *faith and *love. Hope is a positive expectation of some future good that is not yet present and where there is some uncertainty, at least about the time when that good will be realized. Hope seems epistemologically weaker than *belief, since one can hope for an event that one does not believe will occur. Some philosophers have proposed that hope might replace belief as a key element in faith, making faith easier to justify as reasonable. Biblically, however, it appears that faith and hope are linked. We hope for the coming of God's kingdom because of our trust in God, and this trust includes beliefs about God's reality and goodness as well as beliefs about God's actions in Jesus.

humanism. A view that assigns a special place and value to human beings and their activities and achievements. Originally, the term was used to denote a movement associated with the development and flourishing of the humanities—those disciplines that deal with human nature and human achievements, such as literature, philosophy and the arts. In the nineteenth century, however, the term was co-opted by Auguste Comte for his "religion of humanity," which he developed as a secular replacement for traditional religious faith. The term continues to be used in this way, as in the *Humanist Manifesto*. However, there is also a rich tradition of Christian humanism. Many Christian humanists are convinced that only in a religious *worldview is the value of human life really understood and safeguarded.

Hume, David (1711-1776). Scottish philosopher who was one of the preeminent thinkers of the *Enlightenment. Hume was an empiricist who claimed that all knowledge of "matters of fact" (any knowledge not grounded in the meanings of terms) is based on sense experience. (*See* empiricism.) Hume developed powerful arguments that our knowledge of cause and effect and reliance on *inductive reasoning are not in themselves rationally justifiable but are based on "custom." In *philosophy of religion, Hume is famous, first, for his argument that belief in *miracles is irrational because the evidence of past experience will always outweigh the testimony in favor of miracles, and second, for a powerful critique of *natural theology in his *Dialogues Concerning Natural Religion*.

Husserl, Edmund (1859-1938). German philosopher who was the founder of *phenomenology and a teacher of Martin *Heidegger. Phenomenology is the attempt to develop a philosophy that describes experience as it is lived, prior to any scientific theorizing that grows out of that experience. Husserl taught that *consciousness is "intentional" and that it can be described both with respect to its subjective act and with respect to the object of its intention, both of which are present in a unified way in experience. There is an irony present in Husserl's project: whereas his major passion was to make philosophy a rigorous science that would allow it to become a foundational discipline for all the other sciences, his major influence has been on existentialist and poststructuralist philosophers who reject that ideal and think of philosophy as hermeneutical. (*See* existentialism; hermeneutics; structuralism.)

I

I-thou relationship. Martin *Buber's term for a special relationship that is possible between persons when those persons relate to each other in a fully personal way and do not think of the other as an object to be manipulated or as a means to an end. Buber believed that such relationships make possible a different kind of knowledge of the other and that it is possible to have such a relation with God, who is the absolute Thou.

Ibn Rushd. *See* Averroës.

Ibn Sina, Abu Ali. *See* Avicenna.

icons. Images of Christ and the saints often found in Eastern Orthodox churches. The term is also used in a broader sense to designate the capacity of human beings to image God and to become images of Christ. *See also* image of God.

idealism. In *philosophy, a system of thought that takes Mind or Ideas to be ultimate reality, often denying the reality of the physical world as physical altogether or assigning material reality a lesser status. Examples include the following: George *Berkeley's phenomenalism, which views material objects as collections of mental sensations; G. W. F. *Hegel's philosophy of Spirit, which views the whole of reality as the expression of an Absolute Mind; and *Plato's hierarchical view of reality, which views the Forms or Ideas as ultimately real and the material objects as comprising a less real "copy" of the Ideal world. In nonphilosophical contexts, *idealism* often refers to any movement with high ideals—a movement that is intent on improving the world and believes in that possibility.

identity, personal. That which makes a person to be numerically the same individual over time. Theories of personal identity divide into three kinds: (1) psychological theories, which hold that memory or some other psychological continuity constitutes personal identity; (2) bodily theories, which hold that having the same body makes a person to be identical; and (3) nonreductionist theories, which hold that personal identity is either something ultimate and unanalyzable or else that it is grounded in a nonphysical *self that is similarly ultimate. This philosophical debate has direct implications for the possibility of life after death in various forms, such as disembodied *immortality, *reincarnation and *resurrection of the body. *See also* personhood.

image of God. The unique aspects of human persons that allow them to mirror God. This concept is derived from Genesis 1:26, in which Adam and Eve are described as created in the image of God. Theologians have debated whether the image of God has been lost or merely damaged by *sin. They have debated, in addition, whether the image consists of a set of properties (such as rationality and the capacity for responsible action) or is rather to be seen in our relationality (since the Genesis passage links the image of God to being created male and female) or perhaps even consists of our special relation to God.

imago Dei. See image of God.

immortality. That which exists forever or (more loosely) that which has no end. Most theologians think that only God is immortal in the sense of having no beginning or end, though many understand God's immortality not as being temporally everlasting but as being outside *time altogether. Many religions (and philosophers such as *Plato) have believed that humans are immortal in the sense of having no end because they have immaterial souls that survive the death of the body. Christians do not necessarily accept the Platonic view that human souls are intrinsically immortal, but many have thought that the human *soul does continue to exist between death and the *resurrection by virtue of God's power. On this view, humans have a kind of conditional immortality that is dependent on God. *See also* eternity/everlasting; timelessness.

immutability. The *divine attribute of being unchangeable. Many classical theists have held that God's immutability is strict and absolute, since God is atemporal. More recently, some who accept the idea of God as everlasting have argued that although God's basic character and nature do not change, God's experiences are successive and thus God can experience change. (*See* eternity/everlasting; timelessness.) More radically still, some process theologians hold that God's own nature is evolving. (*See* process theology.)

impassibility. The attribute of God's being unaffected by anything outside of himself. Those who accept the view that God is impassible hold that he cannot be caused to do or feel anything, because of his *omnipotence and *perfection. Critics believe that impassibility would be a barrier to genuine loving relations between God and his creatures. *See also* divine attributes.

incarnation. Literally, "enfleshment" or "embodiment." In Christian *theology this term refers to the act whereby God became human in the person of Jesus of Nazareth. The incarnation is logically tied to the doctrine of the *Trinity, as it is God the Son—the second person of the Trinity—who "emptied himself" and became human. (*See* kenotic theories.) The incarnation received a classical formulation at the Council of Chalcedon (451), which said that in becoming human God the Son remained "one person" but had "two natures" (divine and human). *See also* Christology.

incorporeality. The attribute of having no body. Classical Christian theology holds this to be one of the *divine attributes. Some thinkers believe that it is a property of *angels as well. Incorporeality is compatible with the temporary assumption of a bodily appearance, as in the Old Testament theophanies in which God appeared to Abraham and others. Those who hold this to be an essential divine attribute have adopted a variety of explanations as to how the *incarnation is possible.

inductive reasoning. In a strict sense, reasoning to a generalization on the basis of particular instances of that generalization. An example would be the following: "This swan is white; the next swan is white; and so is the next one. Therefore swans are white." With the exception of mathematical induction, where the premises of the argument do necessarily imply their conclusion, inductive arguments do not lead to certainty. In a broader sense, inductive reasoning is any form of reasoning in which the conclusion is not logically entailed by the premises (or in other words, any form of reasoning other than deductive reasoning). Inferences from effect to cause or from cause to effect, and probabilistic inferences in general, are inductive arguments. *See also* deductive argument.

ineffability. That which cannot be expressed in intelligible language. Many mystics have claimed that an experience of God is ineffable (though that has not stopped them from attempting to describe the experience). *See also* mysticism; religious experience.

inerrancy. The doctrine that the Bible is completely trustworthy and contains no errors. The doctrine is normally qualified in a number of ways. The Bible is said to be inerrant in the original autographs, and it is said to be without error only when properly interpreted. Proper interpretation itself requires attention to genre (such as poetry, proverbs and history) and answers to questions about the intentions of the author and conventions shared by author and reader. Some Christians affirm a limited inerrancy, declaring that the lack of error holds only for certain types of truth that God intends to reveal through Scripture, primarily matters of morality and theology. *See also* infallibility.

infallibility. The characteristic of being completely trustworthy, incapable of erring or failing to accomplish an intended purpose. Protestants normally apply this characteristic to the Bible; Catholics extend infallibility to the *magisterium (teaching authority) of the church. If one assumes that a purpose of the Bible is to communicate revealed truth, then infallibility logically implies at least limited *inerrancy. Nevertheless, in practice some theologians affirm the infallibility but not the inerrancy of the Scriptures, intending thereby to indicate that the Bible can be relied on as an *authority in matters of faith and practice while recognizing the possibility of scientific and historical errors.

inference to the best explanation. Type of reasoning in which the truth of a theory or proposition is affirmed on the grounds that it best accounts for all of the available evidence. This type of inference is sometimes called "abduction" by those who think it is a type of reasoning distinct from induction and deduction. (*See* deductive argument; inductive reasoning.) Inference to the best explanation is common in daily life, the detective story and science. Advocates of *cumulative case apologetics typically appeal to this kind of argument pattern in arguing for the existence of God.

infinity. The characteristic of having no bounds or limits. In classical theism, many of God's attributes, such as knowledge, power and love, are viewed as infinite. (*See* attributes of God.) In set theory, *infinite* is often defined as the property of a set that has a subset whose members can be placed in a one-to-one correspondence with the original set, as is the case for the natural numbers and the even integers. With respect to a series, there is debate among philosophers as to whether an actual infinite is possible, as opposed to a procedure that can in principle be repeated endlessly. Those who deny an actual infinite must also deny that the universe is infinitely old.

inspiration. The characteristic of being filled and led by the Spirit of God. Thus the Old Testament prophets are regarded as having spoken by inspiration. Many Christian theologians claim that the Bible is the result of divine inspiration as well, adding that this is the reason it is inerrant or infallible. (*See* inerrancy; infallibility.) The relation between divine inspiration and the human authorship of the Bible has been variously conceived, but generally an affirmation of inspiration is not intended to deny that the human characteristics of the authors shaped the text in various ways.

intelligent design. The scientific hypothesis that the natural order contains a type of complexity that requires an intelligent designer as a cause. Such advocates of intelligent design as Philip Johnson, Michael Behe and William Dembski think that intelligent design is a concept that can support an empirical research program. The intelligent design movement is not necessarily committed to young-earth *creationism and does not insist from a scientific perspective that the hypothesized designer must be identical with the God of the Bible. See also Darwinism; evolution, theory of; teleological argument.

Irenaeus (c. 130-200). A church father who wrote in Greek against the Gnostic heresies of the day. (See Gnosticism.) Irenaeus is known for his argument that Christ came to actualize all those perfections that God had intended humans to have but that were lost through the sin of Adam and Eve. (See Fall, the.) He is also known for having inspired a "soul-making" *theodicy, which justifies suffering as part of the process whereby humans become all they can be.

Islam. Monotheistic religion that originated in what is today Saudi Arabia in the seventh century as a result of the prophetic teachings of Muhammad, recorded in the Qur'an. Islam emphasizes submission to Allah (God) and accepts *Judaism and Christianity as partially true, grounded in earlier revelations from God. In the medieval period Islam provided a congenial environment for the *philosophy of religion. See also Islamic philosophy.

Islamic philosophy. The intellectual product of Islamic thinkers such as al-Farabi, *Avicenna and *Averroës, who creatively synthesized the monotheistic faith of the Qur'an with the Greek philosophical thought of *Plato and *Aristotle in the early Middle Ages. These thinkers grappled with such questions as the nature of *creation and the relation of God to the world and the compatibility of human freedom and divine *sovereignty. See also Islam.

J

Jainism. One of the religions of India, distinguished from *Hinduism by its refusal to accept the Brahmanic Vedas as authoritative. Jainism grew out of the teachings of Mahavira, a fifth-century B.C. contemporary of Gautama (the Buddha). It is distinguished by its emphasis on asceticism and commitment to the principle of harmlessness.

James, William (1842-1910). American philosopher and psychologist and one of the originators of *pragmatism. In *philosophy of religion James is known for his argument in "The Will to Believe" that *faith can be reasonable even if it is not supported by the preponderance of evidence. (*See* will to believe.) He is known as well for his astute descriptions of the religious life in *The Varieties of Religious Experience*.

Judaism. The religion of the Jewish people that takes the Hebrew Bible (regarded by Christians as the Old Testament) as authoritative. Judaism exists in various forms—Orthodox, Conservative and Reformed—and each form interprets biblical *authority somewhat differently. This religion takes as its starting point the special vocation of the Jewish people, called out of Egypt and led by Moses, as those to whom God's law was given. Judaism has nurtured a centuries-old tradition in *philosophy, ranging from Philo in the first century through such medieval thinkers as Moses *Maimonides to many distinguished contemporary Jewish philosophers.

judgment, last. Final assessment by God of the works and *character of humans. Christians believe that the saving work of Christ provides the only hope for humans to stand in the day of judgment. *See also* retribution.

just war theory. The ethical theory that Christians may legitimately fight in wars, but only when certain conditions are met. Those conditions include the following: the cause must be just; the war must be waged by a legitimate government; the means used must be moral; the war must be a last resort; and there must be a reasonable chance of achieving the goals of the war.

The just war theory has been the dominant view about participation in war among Catholic, Lutheran and Reformed theologians. It has traditionally been rejected by Mennonites, Quakers and members of other peace churches. Today it is increasingly questioned in the traditions that have nurtured it, especially with respect to the possibility of a nuclear conflict. *See also* pacifism.

justice. Giving people what is due them. As a social ideal, justice is a major concept in political philosophy. Traditional philosophers also saw justice as a personal *virtue and inquired about the nature of a just person as well as how a person acquires a just *character. In contemporary society there is much dispute about the nature of economic justice, retributive justice and political justice. Theological questions about justice are posed by doctrines such as *predestination and *hell understood as eternal punishment.

justification. A positive term of appraisal in epistemology, used in a variety of ways. A belief is said to be justified deontologically when the believer has adequately fulfilled his or her epistemic duties in acquiring and maintaining the belief. A belief is said to be justified in a more substantive sense when it is based on a good reason, or has the right kind of ground or foundation, one that makes it likely or more likely that the belief is *true*. Justification in epistemology obviously must be distinguished from justification in theology, where the term refers to God's action in accepting Jesus' atonement as sufficient to warrant the acceptance of human beings as righteous even while they are still sinful.

Justin Martyr (c. 105–c. 165). One of the early church fathers who saw positive value in philosophy for Christianity. Justin believed that Greek *philosophy contained truths due to the work of the *Logos—Christ understood as the Creator who works in all people.

K

kalam cosmological argument. Version of the first-cause argument for God's reality, developed by Islamic thinkers, which claims that the world must have had a beginning and that God must exist as the cause of that beginning. Defended in the twentieth century by William Craig. *See also* cosmological arguments; Islamic philosophy; theistic arguments.

Kant, Immanuel (1724-1804). One of the greatest modern philosophers, whose critical philosophy attempted to synthesize the insights of both *rationalism and *empiricism. Kant argued in his *Critique of Pure Reason* that genuine scientific knowledge is possible but that this knowledge is of "phenomenal" reality—that is, reality as it appears to us, rather than reality as it is in itself. Human knowledge is always structured by space and time, which are the "forms of intuition" of the human mind, and by the categories provided by the human understanding such as causality and substance. As Kant saw it, though traditional *natural theology is a failure and no theoretical knowledge of God is possible, recognizing the limits of reason allows room for a rational, moral faith. As we strive to live morally in accordance with the *categorical imperative, we must rationally presuppose human freedom, the existence of God and *immortality.

kenotic theories. Theories of the *incarnation, inspired by Philippians 2:7 (from Greek *kenoō,* "to empty") and other New Testament passages, which hold that in becoming human God the Son divested himself (at least temporarily) of some of the *divine attributes, such as *omnipotence, *omniscience and *omnipresence. Kenotic theories of the incarnation have led some to develop kenotic theories of the nature of God, which view the essence of God to be his self-giving love that freely limits itself to allow some *autonomy to his creation.

Kierkegaard, Søren (1813-1855). Danish Christian philosopher and theologian, whose writings contain a stinging critique of G. W. F. *Hegel and *idealism, *liberal theology, and the whole culture of Christendom, which assumes that we are all Christians by virtue of being Danes, Americans or whatever. Kierkegaard considered himself to be a missionary whose vocation was to reintroduce Christianity into Christendom. His philosophical work focuses on the nature of human existence, since he thought that Christianity must first be understood as a way of existing but that people have forgotten what it means to exist as a human being. Kierkegaard rejected apologetic attempts to make Christianity appear reasonable, holding that New Testament Christianity must always appear foolish to the worldly mind and that genuine proclamation of the gospel always maintains the possibility of offense. He stressed the qualitative difference between God and human beings and viewed the *incarnation as an absolute paradox that human *reason cannot understand but can only believe in *faith.

knowledge. True *belief that is warranted or justified. A person cannot know what is false, but a mere true belief that is the result of luck or guessing does not appear to constitute knowledge either. Most philosophers therefore agree that knowledge requires a true belief that is justified or warranted or that has been acquired through a reliable process, though there is great disagreement as to what it is that warrants or justifies a belief.

L

language, religious (theories of). Accounts of how human language can be used meaningfully to refer to and communicate information about a transcendent God. In the medieval period thinkers developed subtle theories of analogy. (*See* analogical predication.) In the mid-twentieth century *logical positivists challenged the cognitive meaningfulness of religious language and inspired a debate about the verifiability or falsifiability of such language. In the last half of the twentieth century Ludwig *Wittgenstein's work on "language games" attracted much attention to the unique character of religious language and its relation to various forms of life.

law (moral, divine, natural). A rule prescribed by a controlling *authority. The laws of a state or nation typically regulate conduct or behavior. Believers in God typically think of laws in several distinct, though overlapping, senses. The divine law represents God's governing decrees, at least some of which may be knowable only through a *special *revelation from God. Those who accept a *divine command theory of *morality will typically think of the moral law as part of the divine law, with disagreements as to whether the moral law can be known independently of special revelation. Others, particularly nontheists, may use the expression "moral law" metaphorically, to indicate the lawlike force of moral obligations, even though these obligations are not literally issued as laws. The term "natural law" is used to indicate a moral law that God has instituted by virtue of creating the world with particular structures and purposes; to act morally is to act in accord with nature, in ways that respect the natural functions of things. Typically those who affirm *natural law in this sense think of such principles as things that can be ascertained apart from special revelation. "Natural law" in this sense should be distinguished from "laws of nature" understood as scientific or physical laws. Again, theists may think of scientific laws as representing God's ordered rule of creation, while nontheists may use the expression "law" here metaphorically to indicate the regular, lawlike order that *science discovers, without necessarily attributing that order to any intentional design.

Leibniz, Gottfried (1646-1716). German rationalist philosopher who taught that reality is composed of monads—simple substances that have no spatial extension. God is the supreme monad and creates and conserves all other monads. Monads do not really interact with each other but appear to do so due to the "pre-established harmony" that God ordains. Leibniz argued that God could have created any possible world. Because God is perfect, Leibniz concluded that the actual world must be the best possible world. In addition to his many contributions to logic, Leibniz invented calculus (simultaneously with Newton). *See also* rationalism.

Lessing, Gotthold (1729-1781). German philosopher, literary author and critic who developed a historical conception of religion and religious *truth. For Lessing, the great world religions are primarily way stations in the ethical progress of humankind; none is absolutely true. He is famous for his conception of the "ugly, wide ditch" between "eternal truths of reason" and the truths of history. He argued that this logical gap makes it impossible to embrace the historical claims of Christianity with the kind of certainty religion demands. *See also* rationalism.

Levinas, Emmanuel (1906-1995). Jewish philosopher who spent his career in France, though born in Lithuania. Levinas is distinguished by his emphasis on *ethics as "first philosophy" and by his claim that ethics is grounded in a direct experience of the "gaze of the other" rather than theory. Levinas taught that true religion grows out of this same encounter with the Other, in which we discover a God who cannot be viewed as an object.

Lewis, C. S. (1898-1963). Belfast-born English literary critic, novelist and Christian apologist. The popularity and simplicity of Lewis's philosophical *apologetics belie the intellectual depth of his work. His *Mere Christianity* is probably the most successful work of Christian apologetics of the twentieth century, and his Narnia books are beloved by children and adults for their wonderful blend of charm, fantasy and theological insight. Lewis grappled with the problem of *evil in *The Problem of Pain* and with supernaturalism in *Miracles*. *The Abolition of Man* focuses on the importance of emotion and objective moral truths to our understanding of human nature. *See also* mere Christianity.

liberalism (theological). Movement in Protestant *theology since the nineteenth century that is dominated by the goal of modifying Christianity so as to make it consistent with modern culture and science. Liberalism rejects the traditional view of Scripture as an authoritative propositional *revelation from God in favor of a view that sees revelation as a record of the evolving *religious experiences of humankind. It sees Jesus more as ethical teacher and model rather than as divine atoner and redeemer.

liberation theology. A theological movement that developed in Latin America in the 1960s, emphasizing the gospel as a power that liberates oppressed peoples from unjust economic, political and social structures. Liberation theology is rooted in the special concern the Bible shows for the poor, but it has created controversy by sometimes relying on Marxist-inspired analyses of the causes of poverty and oppression. *See also* justice; Marxism.

libertarianism (metaphysical). In *ethics and *metaphysics, the view that human beings sometimes can will more than one possibility. According to this view, a person who freely made a particular choice could have chosen differently, even if nothing about the past prior to the moment of choice had been different. Libertarianism therefore rejects the *compatibilist view that *free will and *determinism are consistent.

libertarianism (political). In political philosophy, the view that individual human freedom is a primary value and that government restrictions on that freedom should be limited to what is necessary for the maintenance of a society that is conducive to freedom. Thus libertarianism offers a justification of state power over against anarchism, but it holds that there is moral justification only for a minimal state sufficient to defend citizens against attack and protect against crime.

life after death. The continuation of conscious personal existence after death. Traditionally, most Christians have taught that the hope for life after death rests on God's promise of the resurrection of the body, though personal existence continues between death and the resurrection in some "intermediate state," in which those who are saved are with God. Such a view implies the existence of a soul that is separable from the body. In the twentieth century some theologians have argued that

Christians should take a "physicalist" view of the human person that identifies the person and the body. Such a view is incompatible with an intermediate state and faces a problem: how is the resurrected bodily person identical to the person who died when there is no soul to provide that identity?

Locke, John (1632-1704). English philosopher who defended *empiricism in *epistemology and a social contract theory of the state. Locke—one of the founders of modern *philosophy—put forward an empiricist epistemology partly as a way of trying to resolve and control bloody religious conflicts. He defended an ethic that requires humans to inspect their *beliefs and try to ensure that they are holding those beliefs with a degree of confidence proportional to the evidence on which they are based. Locke thought that his epistemology could support a reasonable form of Christianity while limiting what he called "enthusiasm." His political thinking stressed the idea that the state is based on a social contract with the citizens and can therefore lose legitimacy if that contract is undermined. This idea was influential on the founding fathers of the United States.

logical positivism. Philosophical movement arising out of the Vienna Circle of philosophers in Austria after World War I. Logical positivism combined the commitment to *empiricism found in nineteenth-century positivism (Comte) with the type of logical analysis found in the work of Bertrand *Russell. It affirmed a verifiability theory of meaning, in which nonanalytic propositions have *cognitive meaning only if they are empirically verifiable. On the basis of this theory, logical positivists asserted metaphysical and theological propositions to be meaningless, and they analyzed ethical propositions as merely having expressive meaning. *See also* language, religious (theories of).

Logos. Greek term for "Word" or "Reason," used in the prologue to John's Gospel: "In the beginning was the Word." The *Logos* is thus a term for the eternal Son of God, the second person of the *Trinity, understood as the agent of divine *creation and the one who "illumines," or enlightens, human beings. Many early church fathers used this concept to justify a positive attitude toward Greek *philosophy on the grounds that those who lacked the biblical *revelation could still attain some truth because of the operation of Christ as the Logos in them.

love. The heart of God's character and, along with *faith and *hope, one of the cardinal *virtues, according to Christianity. Christian theologians often distinguish among different forms of love: erotic love, friendship love and the love for neighbor that most closely resembles God's self-giving love in Jesus, who came down from heaven and sacrificed his life for humans who were in rebellion against God. *See also* agapism.

Luther, Martin (1483-1546). German theologian and father of the Protestant Reformation. The heart of Luther's understanding of the gospel stressed that *salvation was a free work of *grace that is grasped through *faith. Persons are not saved because of any merits they may possess but because the work of Christ is imputed to them by God.

M

MacIntyre, Alasdair (1929-). British-American philosopher best known for his defense of an Aristotelian ethical theory in *After Virtue.* (*See* Aristotle.) MacIntyre gives special emphasis to the role of tradition and "practices" in *ethics, and he attempts to develop a historical understanding of ethics that is not historicist (in the sense of relativistically losing any concern for *truth), with special attention paid to adjudicating the claims of rival traditions. After an early flirtation with *Marxism, MacIntyre has returned to the Christian faith.

magic. Attempts to achieve ends through practices designed to secure the aid of supernatural or occult powers. Traditional theologians have argued that petitionary *prayer is not magic because the one praying does not think of God as an object to be controlled or manipulated. Some contemporary Bible scholars, however, have argued that this distinction is largely political. They say that religious groups label as "magic" the religious practices of which they disapprove. Further, they claim that such things as the *miracles of Jesus should be understood as similar to what is often called magic. However, it is noteworthy that Jesus normally achieved his miracles without the aid of the kinds of rituals associated with magic.

magisterium. The teaching *authority of the Roman Catholic Church. The magisterium consists of the bishops of the Church under the authority of the pope. Catholics sometimes argue that it is a weakness of Protestant Christianity that it lacks a determinate magisterium.

Maimonides, Moses (1135-1204). Spanish-born Jewish philosopher who eventually settled in Cairo after escaping forced conversion to Christianity. Maimonides defended a biblical view of *creation against Aristotelian theories that the world is eternal while at the same time defending a *negative theology that requires a recognition of the anthropomorphic quality of much of the biblical language about God. *See also* Aristotle; anthropomorphism.

Manichaeism. Religious view developed by Manes (c. 216-276), who saw himself as a prophet succeeding Jesus and Zoroaster. Manichaeism competed with Christianity in the late Roman Empire, and no less a person than St. *Augustine went through a Manichaean period on his way to Christianity. Manichaeism is characterized by a dualistic *ontology that sees matter and the physical world as bad, in tension with the pure world of spirit and light. The human task is to gain freedom from the physical world through ascetic practices. *See also* dualism.

Marcel, Gabriel-Honoré (1889-1973). French Catholic philosopher and playwright who represented the religious wing of *existentialism over against Jean Paul *Sartre's *atheism. Marcel emphasized the role of mysteries (which are distinguished from problems) in *philosophy. He saw human existence as a journey and said the ambiguities of human life call forth a response from us that reveals our own *character. "Creative fidelity" is Marcel's term for the response that is crucial to understanding other people and God.

Marx, Karl (1818-1883). Revolutionary German thinker, trained as a social philosopher, who spent much of his life in England writing his major work, *Capital*. Marx was originally a left-wing follower of G. W. F. *Hegel but became a materialist following Ludwig *Feuerbach and "turned Hegel right side up" by applying Hegel's dialectic to an analysis of history as the product of economic class struggle. In his early work Marx used religious and philosophical language, but he substituted economic analysis in his later writings. His *Communist Manifesto*, coauthored with Friedrich Engels, was a seminal document in the development of communism.

Marxism. Revolutionary philosophical movement founded by Karl *Marx and Friedrich Engels. Marxism sees economic factors as determinative in history, with social class struggles shaped by the means of production that characterize a given economic system. Further, Marxism sees capitalism as nearing the end of history, since under capitalism human productivity has increased so much that the elimination of human need is possible for the first time. Marx predicted that capitalism will collapse because it creates an ever-increasing class of propertyless workers (the proletariat). As wealth is centered in a small number of capitalists, overproduction, due to the lack of purchasing power by the masses, will become a crisis. Eventually, the workers will overthrow the system, creating a dictatorship of the proletariat that will progressively eliminate the state as social classes disappear. Ironically, the countries where revolutionary movements committed to Marxism have succeeded have been relatively backward countries such as Russia and China. Though communism as a revolutionary movement seems a spent force, Marxism as a philosophical theory is still influential in the academy.

materialism. The view that only material objects exist. *Materialism* is sometimes used as a synonym for *physicalism*, but some thinkers distinguish the two by allowing that *physicalism holds that only matter and energy exist. Some materialists define their view in terms of *science and claim that ultimate reality consists of whatever particles or entities are discovered by physicists. *See also* eliminative materialism; nonreductive materialism.

mere Christianity. Term used by C. S. *Lewis (in a book with the same title) for those essential Christian beliefs shared by all branches of historic Christianity—Eastern Orthodox, Catholic and Protestant. Lewis did not think that a person could be a "mere Christian," since all Christians must hold a fuller, more concrete version of their faith. He saw the various branches of Christianity as rooms to be lived in, while mere Christianity is something like a corridor or vestibule that all these rooms share in common. For example, a belief in the *atonement would be part of mere Christianity; a specific theory of how the atonement occurred would not be.

metaethics. The branch of *ethics that focuses on the meanings of fundamental ethical concepts, the justification of ethical claims and the metaphysical status of ethical entities. Metaethics is usually contrasted with normative ethics, which deals directly with what is good and right, and applied ethics, which deals with the application of normative principles to such specific fields as medicine and law.

metaphor. A term or phrase that normally refers to one thing but is used in an unusual way, so that it now has a different referent and may have an unusual sense as well. Metaphors thus are used to suggest some kind of likeness or similarity between two things that might not immediately be seen as alike. There is much argument about the nature of metaphor, but increasingly philosophers agree that metaphors are essential to cognitive advances in *science as well as religion and are not merely adornment that can be replaced by literal language. *See also* language, religious (theories of).

metaphysics. The branch of philosophy that deals with the nature of reality. Literally, metaphysics is that which is "beyond" or "after" physics, since it deals with questions such as the following: Are the entities postulated by science real? Does God exist? Do numbers and other mathematical objects exist independently of the human mind? The term is sometimes used pejoratively, to designate an attempt to develop an impossible "super science" that would achieve completeness and certainty. It is also used as a synonym for *ontology*, the name for the study of being. *See also* ontology.

middle knowledge. Knowledge of those propositions now called "counterfactuals of freedom," which deal with how a being who possesses libertarian freedom would act in any particular situation. (*See* counterfactuals; libertarianism [metaphysical].) It is middle knowledge in contrast to knowledge of propositions about what is the case, on the one hand, and knowledge of propositions about what is possibly or necessarily true, on the other. The sixteenth-century philosopher Luis de Molina attributed this kind of knowledge to God, and the view that God has such knowledge is often called Molinism. If God has middle knowledge, then it would be possible for him to create a certain world and know how creatures would act in that world without limiting their freedom. Thus proponents of Molinism believe that this view resolves the difficulty as to how God can know with necessity what humans will freely choose. *See also* determinism; foreknowledge, divine; free will.

mind-body problem. The metaphysical problem about the nature of the mind and its relation to the body. Called by philosopher Arthur Schopenhauer (1788-1860) the "world-knot" because of its ties to so many of the central problems in philosophy, the mind-body problem remains a major mystery. Most secular philosophers today espouse some form of *materialism, which rejects the existence of the mind or soul as a separate, nonphysical entity. However, there is little agreement as to which form of materialism is successful or how materialism can account for such phenomena as *consciousness and the "intentionality" or referential dimension of mental states (the power of mental states, such as beliefs, hopes and fears, to be *about* something else, as when I believe *that* God exists or hope *for* the second coming). Traditional religious views that affirm life after death have usually opted for some form of *dualism, which would seem to make possible both a disembodied afterlife (on some conceptions of the soul or mind) and a resurrected afterlife, in which the soul enlivens or animates a new body. Materialists who hold to a resurrected afterlife must hold that the new body is identical to the body that died, a problematic claim.

miracle. An event brought about by a special act of God. There is much disagreement about the definition beyond this minimum. Some thinkers argue that a miracle must involve an exception to the laws of nature or (perhaps alternatively) involve some event that exceeds the natural powers or capacities of natural things. Others insist that a miracle is recognizable primarily by its revelatory power as a sign that shows something about God or God's purposes and that such events do not have to be scientifically inexplicable. Since David *Hume's famous attack on miracles, the possibility of miracles and the kind of evidence needed for belief in miracles has been subject to debate. Traditional *apologetics viewed miracles as important confirmation or certification that a prophet or apostle was genuinely sent by God. *See also* divine action.

model. A representation—which may consist of a physical structure or collection of objects, a picture, or a collection of abstract entities—that has a systematic relation to that which it represents. Typically this requires one to be able to translate or map both the elements of what is represented and their relationships into the model. The model is usually in some way simpler than what is modeled and thus leads to greater understanding. In mathematics a model requires a precisely defined formal relationship. Using computers, researchers often simulate or provide a model for some complex phenomenon such as a weather system. In philosophy of science the term can be used loosely, as when we speak of a model of an atom as a kind of miniature solar system, or more strictly, which requires a mathematical account of the relation between the model and what is represented. Theologians have extended the concept of model by arguing that even though God is infinite and transcendent, models of aspects of his reality and activity may be provided that increase our understanding. Just as is the case in science, such models necessarily simplify and fail to represent fully the reality they intend to represent, but they nevertheless can give insight and helpful guidance.

modernism. A movement to modify Christianity to make it relevant and acceptable to modern peoples, emphasizing both science and social and political teachings. Modernism is closely linked with theological *liberalism, but while liberalism is more exclusively tied to Protestantism, modernism enjoyed favor among Catholic intellectuals at the end of the nineteenth century and beginning of the twentieth. *See also* postmodernism.

Molinism. *See* middle knowledge.

monism. The *metaphysical view that reality is fundamentally one. The monist thus holds that the plurality of objects we seem to experience is merely appearance or is less than fully real. Monism is often linked to Absolute *Idealism and certain forms of *Hinduism, chiefly *Advaita Vedanta.

monotheism. *See* theism.

moral arguments (for God's existence). Arguments that God must exist as the ground of the moral order (or some aspect of that order, such as moral obligations) or as the explanation of certain moral facts. For example, some have argued that moral obligations consist of *laws and that such laws require a Lawgiver. *See also* theistic arguments.

morality. The system of rules that ideally should govern human behavior with respect to right and wrong, *good and *evil. Morality is roughly synonymous with *ethics, though some take ethics to be broader in its compass (including reflection on the nature of the good life, for example) and some think that a distinctive feature of morality (but not ethics) is its demand for so-called "public reasons" for moral rules. There are certainly disagreements among cultures and within cultures as to which moral rules are valid and binding. Some conclude from this disagreement that morality itself is relative and not objective. (*See* relativism.) Yet some disagreement about the content of morality is consistent with the existence of objective moral standards.

mystery. That which surpasses the comprehensibility of human *reason. In *theology the mysteries of faith are revealed truths, regarded as above reason but not contrary to reason, though perhaps contrary to human expectations.

mysticism. The view that it is possible to gain experiential knowledge of that which transcends the limits of human *reason and sensory *perception. When associated with a religious tradition (as is usually the case), the mystic holds that it is possible to gain an awareness of God or ultimate reality through certain kinds of experiences, which are often claimed to be *ineffable. Theists interpret such experiences as making possible a special intimacy or oneness with God but deny the *monistic claim that in such experiences the mystic becomes aware of an identity with God.

N

natural law. Moral principles supposed to govern human behavior that can be recognized independently of *special *revelation. Advocates of natural law typically think that at least the basic principles of natural law are knowable by all people and thus can be said to be "written on the heart." The natural law tradition links *morality to the "natures" things possess and the purposes of those natures. Theists think of natural laws as literal *laws promulgated by God, though some naturalists who believe in natural laws use the term metaphorically.

natural light. Metaphorical way of describing the power of *reason to discern some *truths as certain on an *a priori basis. René *Descartes, in particular, described those truths that are self-evident (clear and distinct to human reason) as truths that we know by "natural light." This metaphor is partly a survival of the strong emphasis in the medieval period on *knowledge as the result of the divine illumination of the mind.

natural theology. The discipline that attempts to gain *knowledge of God apart from any *special *revelation from God. Natural theologians have typically tried to infer God's existence through *theistic arguments such as the *cosmological and *teleological arguments as well as by reflecting on generic human experience. Catholic theology has traditionally affirmed the value of natural theology, while many Protestants, especially from the *Reformed tradition, have been less enthusiastic about its prospects.

naturalism. The philosophical theory that nature is all that exists. Naturalists typically deny the existence of *God, *angels and *demons and are skeptical of the possibility of life after death.

nature/grace relationship. The relation between the natural order and God's redemptive work in Christ. Catholics, particularly in the medieval period, tended to think that "grace presupposes nature and perfects it" (in Thomas *Aquinas's words). Some Reformation thinkers were suspicious of this formula on the grounds that it does not fully recognize the fallenness of the natural order. (*See* Fall, the.) This question is particularly important for *ethics and the question as to whether Christian ethics presupposes an ethic of *natural law or rather must be understood as a distinct system of ethical thinking.

necessary being. A being whose existence is no mere accident or contingent result but whose very nature is to exist necessarily. God has traditionally been understood as a necessary being, and it is this aspect of the concept of *God that underlies the *ontological argument for God's existence. A necessary being can be defined (following Gottfried *Leibniz) as one that exists in every possible world. *See also* necessity.

necessary truths. Those propositions whose falsehood is logically impossible. A necessary truth can be understood (following Gottfried *Leibniz) as one that is true in every possible world. (Similarly, contingent propositions are true in at least one possible world; necessarily false propositions are true in no possible world.) *See also* necessity; truth.

necessity. One of the family of modal properties, along with possibility and impossibility, attributed to propositions, beings and properties. (*See* necessary being; necessary truths.) A being possesses a property by necessity if there is no possible world in which that being could exist without having that property. A property that is possessed by necessity is also said to be an essence of the object that possesses it, since its presence is essential to that object.

negative theology. A tradition that stresses the *transcendence of God by attempting to understand God by those properties that God does not have. In this tradition God is described by denying to him the finite properties of other objects. God is thus not dependent on anything, not limited by a body or by time, not limited in knowledge or power. Negative theology is often linked to *mysticism, which is alleged to provide the *ineffable experiences that give us the glimmerings of a positive conception of God.

neo-orthodoxy. Early- to mid-twentieth-century theological movement associated with such Protestant theologians as Karl *Barth and Emil *Brunner. Neo-orthodoxy criticized *liberalism for diminishing the *transcendence of God and the importance of divine *revelation. Neo-orthodox theologians frequently argued for a dialectical theology that held contrasting emphases, such as divine sovereignty and human freedom, together in tension.

Neo-Platonism. One of the schools of Hellenistic *philosophy, loosely inspired by *Plato. *Plotinus (205-270) was the seminal figure and most famous representative of Neo-Platonism. Neo-Platonism emphasizes that all of reality emanates through a hierarchical series from the One, the Form of the Good, and that it is destined to return to the One. This philosophy's tendencies toward the depreciation of matter and cultivation of ascetic practices made a strong impact on many of the church fathers. *See also* chain of being; idealism.

Newman, Cardinal John Henry (1801-1890). English theologian, philosopher of religion and church leader. As a young man, Newman was a leader of the Oxford (or Tractarian) movement, which inspired the present-day tradition of high-church or "Catholic" Anglicanism. However, in 1845 Newman converted to Roman Catholicism, later became a priest and eventually was made a cardinal. In *The Grammar of Assent* Newman described the kind of informal reasoning, sensitive to concrete experience, that often is present in human thinking and that he saw as fundamental to religious reasoning.

Nietzsche, Friedrich (1844-1900). German philosopher whose radical views on human thinking as perspectival and shaped by the "will to power" have had a profound impact on thinkers who came after him. Nietzsche announced the death of God, and as a consequence he affirmed that moralities are human creations. Previous human history has seen the "slave revolt" in *morality, in which the "herd morality" of good and evil (Judaism, Christianity, socialism) has overthrown the earlier "master morality" of good and bad (the warrior culture of Homeric Greece) that was the work of the natural aristocrats. Nietzsche himself proposed that the "Overman" may now go beyond good and evil and invent a new form of morality. Nietzsche saw the virtues of herd morality as a disguised form of envy, in which the weak express their resentment of the strong by affirming that the poor and the meek are blessed. *See also* nihilism.

nihilism. The rejection of objective moral values and structures, literally "nothingism." The nihilist is a skeptic about moral traditions and obligations and does not regard them as binding. A distinction should be made between the attitude of the reluctant or sorrowing nihilist, who finds nihilism terrifying but true, and the celebrative nihilist, who views nihilism as liberation from oppressive rules. Friedrich *Nietzsche is often mentioned in discussions of nihilism, partly because of his own ambivalence. Nietzsche sometimes described nihilism as a fate that haunts Western culture. At other times he seems more celebrative in his calls for the construction of a new morality. For

those who believe morality requires a transcendent basis,
Nietzsche's philosophy appears nihilistic, but for naturalists
who think that humans can themselves provide a basis for morality, Nietzsche is seen as a guide pointing beyond nihilism.

nominalism. The claim that universal terms such as *goodness*,
justice and *fatherhood* are merely names and do not denote any
objective, universal qualities. Thus the nominalist holds a view
opposite to that of the Platonic realist who accepts the independent reality of universals. (*See* antirealism; conceptualism;
Plato; realism.) Nominalism typically holds that universal
terms are used to denote a plurality of individuals who are
grouped together by the mind because of perceptions of similarity. This requires the claim that two things can be similar
without sharing in common some universal property.

noncognitivism. The theory that certain propositions, such as
those of morality and religion, are neither true nor false and
therefore lack *cognitive meaning. Noncognitivist theories in
*ethics include emotivism, which holds that ethical proposi-
tions express emotional attitudes rather than make true or
false statements, and prescriptivism, which holds that moral
propositions such as "Telling the truth is morally right" are
disguised imperatives and have the force of "Tell the truth!"
Noncognitivism in religion holds that religious propositions
are similarly devoid of any truth or falsity. For example, a person who affirms life after death does not mean to affirm any
fact about what will happen beyond the grave but might rather
be expressing a certain attitude toward life.

nonreductive materialism. Term used for a view of the human
person that rejects *mind-body *dualism but affirms that even
though a person is a material object he or she cannot be understood solely in physical terms. Typically, nonreductive materialists believe that there are certain high-level properties, such
as being kind or being thoughtful, that supervene on a person's physical properties without being reducible to those
properties. The notion of supervenience can be understood in
different ways, but typically its advocates say that the under-

lying physical properties are necessary for the higher-level properties, but those higher properties require concepts that cannot be reduced to concepts on the more basic physical level. One example of nonreductive materialism is a view holding that persons are composed of their bodies without being identical to those bodies. *See also* materialism.

numinous. An aspect of *religious experience discussed by Rudolf Otto in *The Idea of the Holy.* Otto described a type of religious experience typically associated with *theism in which God is experienced as "wholly other"—a mysterious, awesome, fascinating object. The majesty and holiness of God produce a sense of awe, dependence and even fear on the part of the subject of the experience.

O

objectivity. The quality of a fair-minded inquirer concerned about *truth. The nature of this quality is, however, controversial. One ideal of objectivity is that of the completely neutral, detached, emotionless, presuppositionless thinker, who occupies what Thomas Nagel has called "the view from nowhere" or sees the world as Baruch *Spinoza described it, from a godlike viewpoint, "under the aspect of eternity." Objectivity in this sense is widely attacked by *postmodern thinkers as an impossible and even undesirable ideal. However, objectivity in this sense should be distinguished from the honesty of the person who really cares about truth and is willing to respect contrary evidence. This kind of objectivity seems compatible with recognizing our human *finitude and the ways in which our passions and assumptions can function as aids in the search for truth, rather than simply being distorting filters. *See also* relativism; subjectivism.

Ockham, William of (c. 1285-1349). English medieval philosopher known as "the subtle doctor." Ockham was a Franciscan who clashed with the pope and was forced to flee to Pisa and finally Munich because of his criticisms of arbitrary papal power. He is known for his rejection of real universals and is often called the father of *nominalism, although many scholars claim that he was really a *conceptualist. Ockham is also famous for "Ockham's razor," or the principle of parsimony, which says that "entities should not be multiplied beyond necessity." Though that phrase is not actually found in Ockham's writings, it is associated with him because of his characteristic style of philosophizing.

omnibenevolence. The quality of being completely *good. Omnibenevolence is one of the traditional *attributes of God and is thought to be necessarily possessed by a God who is perfect.

omnipotence. The quality of being all-powerful, normally understood as the power to perform any *action that is logically possible and consistent with God's essential nature. Omnipotence is one of the traditional *attributes of God. Many attempts to analyze this property have been made, centering on the "paradox of the stone"—a vivid illustration of the logical difficulties raised by omnipotence. The paradox of the stone begins with the question "Can God create a stone that he cannot move?" If so, there is something God cannot do (move the stone). But if God cannot create such a stone, then there also appears to be something God cannot do. The source of the paradox is the question as to whether it is possible for an omnipotent being to limit itself.

omnipresence. The quality of being present at all places—one of the traditional *attributes of God. Those who believe God is atemporal extend this concept and think of God as present at all times. (*See* eternity/everlasting; timelessness.) Traditional theists do not think of God as spatially located at all and therefore do not think of omnipresence as a ubiquitous physical presence but as God's being present at all places by virtue of his knowledge and power to act. God is aware of what is happening at every place and has the power to act directly at any place.

omniscience. The quality of being all-knowing. This is one of the traditional *attributes of God. Omniscience is usually analyzed as knowing the *truth value of every proposition. Controversy has centered around the compatibility of divine *foreknowledge with human *free will, though many defend the claim that there is no inconsistency. (*See* compatibilism; middle knowledge.) However, some argue that God's omniscience does not extend to all future *actions, either because the propositions about such actions are as yet neither true nor false or else because it is logically impossible to know their truth.

ontological argument. *A priori argument for God's existence holding that the concept of God implies his necessary existence. (*See* necessary being.) *Anselm is credited with originating this argument with his claim that God is a being "than which none greater can be conceived" and that a being who existed only in thought would not be such a being. The argument was defended by René *Descartes and Gottfried *Leibniz and attacked by David *Hume and Immanuel *Kant. In the twentieth century the argument was defended by Alvin *Plantinga, Norman Malcolm and Charles Hartshorne. Some of the twentieth-century versions stressed the idea that necessary existence is an essential property of God. *See also* theistic arguments.

ontology. The study of being. Ontology is often considered to be equivalent to *metaphysics, but some thinkers, such as Martin *Heidegger, have viewed ontology as a quest to understand the meaning of being, in contrast to metaphysics as inquiry about specific types of entities.

open theism. Theological view claiming that some of the traditional *attributes ascribed to God by classical *theism should be either rejected or reinterpreted. Advocates typically reject the claim that God is timelessly eternal in favor of seeing God as everlasting, and they believe that though God's essential character is immutable, God changes in some ways so as to respond appropriately to a changing creation. (*See* eternity/everlasting; immutability.) Most controversially, open theists typically hold that God's *foreknowledge is limited, because of the limitations he has placed upon himself in giving humans *free will. Open theists argue that their position is more consistent with the biblical picture of God than is classical theism, which they claim distorted the biblical picture because of Greek philosophical concepts of *perfection. Critics charge that open theism does not do justice to divine *sovereignty. Open theism has some similarities to *process theology, but the differences are significant: methodologically, open theists are committed to a high view of biblical *authority; and substantively, they accept the concept of God as a personal agent as well as the miraculous events of the Bible, which are typically rejected by process theologians. Open theists, unlike process theologians, have no particular reason to challenge the traditional conceptual scheme of substances that have properties, some of them essential.

order of being/order of knowing. Medieval distinction between the ontological order and the epistemological order. For example, Thomas *Aquinas believed that God is the ground of existence for all other beings. Hence, in the order of being (*ontology), God is primary. However, humans come to know finite objects through their senses first and must infer the existence of God from God's effects. Thus, in the order of knowing (*epistemology), finite objects precede God.

Origen (c. 185-254). Church father in the Alexandrian church whose writings show the influence of *Plato. One of the first apologists for Christianity, Origen held some views later considered unorthodox, including a belief in the preexistence of human *souls (though not *reincarnation). He also taught a doctrine of eventual *universal salvation and developed a theory of the allegorical interpretation of Scripture.

original sin. The universal sinfulness of the human race (except for Jesus and—for Roman Catholics—Mary) originated by Adam and Eve and transmitted to their posterity. (*See* Fall, the.) Some languages actually use the term *inherited sin* for *original sin*, though it is questionable whether *sin can be inherited. Philosophical problems raised by this doctrine include questions as to the relation of Adam and Eve to later humans and the responsibility and freedom of those later individuals. Some distinguish between the sinfulness or predisposition to sin that is inherited and actual sin.

P

pacifism. The belief that war is unacceptable, either because war is inherently immoral or because Christians are called to a higher standard of conduct. Some pacifists extend their opposition to war to any killing or violence. For Christian theologians the chief alternative to pacifism has been the *just war theory. Pacifism was the dominant view in the early church and is the historic position of such churches as the Mennonites and the Quakers.

paganism. The religious outlook common among pre-Christian peoples in the Middle East and Europe, usually involving *polytheism. The term is also used for tribal religions in other parts of the world and, in a somewhat extended sense, for the post-Christian Western "worship" of money, fame, beauty and other finite goods. Some New Age movements, such as *Wicca, see themselves as reviving pagan perspectives and attitudes.

pain. A sensation of extreme discomfort. Theologically, pain contributes to the problem of *evil, since to some skeptics it seems that a good God would not allow pain into the world (or at least not so much of it). The suffering of animals is a particularly difficult problem for *theodicy, insofar as animal pain cannot be justified by the argument that pain is caused by the misuse of human *free will.

Paley, William (1743-1805). English theologian and philosopher whose version of the argument from design was a prominent aspect of nineteenth-century *natural theology. (*See* teleological argument.) Paley's version includes an extended analogy in which a person who has never before seen a watch finds one and concludes that the mechanism must have been designed by an intelligent being. Paley also developed and defended a Christian version of *utilitarianism.

panentheism. The view that the whole of the universe is included in God but does not exhaust God. The world is not distinct from God, as in *theism, but neither is God identical with the world (*pantheism). Panentheists sometimes think of the universe as the body of God, but they say God transcends his body in much the same way that a person transcends his or her material body. Panentheism is a common position in *process theology.

Pannenberg, Wolfhart (1928-). German Lutheran theologian who has prominently defended the view that the identity of Jesus can be recognized and defended through historical inquiry. (*See* historical Jesus.) Pannenberg is distinctive among contemporary European theologians in the weight he puts on historical apologetic arguments, maintaining that the claims of Jesus to be the Son of God and Messiah are confirmed by the *resurrection as a historical event.

pantheism. The belief that God and the world are identical. The most famous Western defender of pantheism is Baruch *Spinoza, who claimed that God and Nature are two names for the same reality, which has mind and material extension as two of its attributes. The term is also used to describe the absolute *monism of *Advaita Vedanta Hinduism, which holds that the whole of reality is identical with the one Absolute that is God, and that the distinctions we draw between objects are just part of appearances.

paradigm. Model or exemplar. The term was used by Thomas Kuhn in *The Structure of Scientific Revolutions* to refer to a pattern of thinking and explanation embodied in the practices and assumptions that are taken for granted by a particular scientific community. The paradigm of a given scientific community makes possible what Kuhn calls "normal science." Paradigms are not falsifiable in the ordinary way but must be overthrown in a scientific revolution, which makes possible a new paradigm.

parity arguments. A type of argument in which it is shown that a criticism of one view applies equally well to some other view, often to the discomfort of the original critic. In *philosophy of religion, parity arguments are frequently effective in showing that criticisms of religious *belief are really rooted in bad *epistemology. For example, an apologist might try to show how an argument that one cannot reasonably believe in God also implies that it is unreasonable to believe in other minds (as was done by Alvin *Plantinga in *God and Other Minds*). In effect, a parity argument is an application of the proverb "What's sauce for the goose is sauce for the gander."

Pascal, Blaise (1623-1662). French philosopher, mathematician and physicist whose writings about Christianity have had a profound influence. In his posthumously published *Pensées*, Pascal brilliantly analyzed the ambiguities of the human situation and made a case for *belief in a world where human *reason cannot achieve absolute certainty. One argument much discussed is "Pascal's wager," in which he claimed that the eternal *good that may be obtained through *faith in God makes it prudentially rational to opt for faith even if objective certainty cannot be obtained. *See also* wager argument.

patriarchy, matriarchy. A society dominated by fathers or males in general (in the case of patriarchy) or, more rarely, mothers or females in general (matriarchy). Recent feminists have argued that most human cultures have been dominated by patriarchy and that this has shaped such cultural activities as science and philosophy as well as religion in detrimental and often unnoticed ways. *See also* feminism; gender.

Peirce, Charles Sanders (1839-1914). American philosopher generally regarded as the founder of *pragmatism and the inventor of semiotics, or the general theory of *signs. Peirce viewed *beliefs primarily as rules for *action and regarded *doubt as an unsatisfactory, disturbed state. He thus inverted the priority given by René *Descartes to doubt by claiming that one needed a reason to doubt; the mere logical possibility of a mistake is not a sufficient reason. Peirce's ideas were popularized by William *James and John *Dewey.

Pelagianism. The view that the human will has not been totally ruined by *original sin and that it is therefore possible for humans to achieve moral sanctity by human effort. This view is sometimes associated with the view that original sin is transmitted through environmental or cultural means and therefore can be lessened through social improvements. Pelagian views of sin are attributed to Pelagius (c. 345-c. 425), a British monk who was strongly opposed by *Augustine.

perception. The faculty or power by which humans are aware of objects outside of themselves as well as their own bodies. Since ancient times, philosophers have debated the nature of perception and its reliability. Theories of perception can be divided into three types: (1) direct realist views, which hold that objects are directly perceived; (2) representational realist views, which hold that the direct objects of perception are mental events such as images or ideas that represent objects; and (3) idealist views, which hold that perceived objects simply are collections of mental events. (*See* antirealism; idealism; realism.) Though many attempts have been made to argue for the reliability of perception, philosophers such as Thomas *Reid have argued that perception is one of a number of basic human faculties, all of which must be accepted on trust. Recently, William *Alston has argued that claims to perceive God have rough epistemic parity with ordinary perceptual claims. *See also* epistemology.

perfection. That which is completely good and is in no way defective. The concept of perfection has played a dominant role in *philosophical theology, since God is often conceived of as a being who possesses all perfections. Defenders of *immutability argue that a perfect God cannot change, for any change would imply some unrealized potential in God. Some contemporary thinkers, however, argue that such a changeless God is static and therefore less perfect than one who can respond to his creation and form mutual relationships.

personalism. A philosophy that stresses the intrinsic value and irreducibility of persons, making *personhood central to the understanding of reality as a whole. A version of personalism in an idealist form was developed in the late nineteenth and early twentieth centuries at Boston University by Borden Parker Bowne and Edgar Sheffield Brightman. (*See* idealism.) A realistic version was developed by neo-Scholastics such as Etienne Gilson and Jacques Maritain in the mid-twentieth century. (*See* realism.) *See also* identity, personal; self.

personhood. The unique status shared by human beings, angels and God that involves the power to think, act and value. Traditional theories of personhood stress that persons are substances of a rational nature. More contemporary theories emphasize the ability to act and have emotions, and these often link personhood to the ability to use language and relations to other persons. Many debates in *ethics, such as the moral status of the fetus, hinge on views of personhood and on when personhood begins and ends for humans. *See also* identity, personal; personalism; self.

phenomenology. An approach to philosophy originated by Edmund *Husserl (1859-1938) and his followers characterized by an attempt to describe human experience as it is experienced. Though there are large differences between Husserl and some of his followers (Martin *Heidegger and Maurice Merleau-Ponty, for example), all would agree that phenomenology requires a suspension of the natural attitude, which takes the world of objects for granted and looks at experience as caused by objects, so as to enable a focus on the "life-world" of experience. Phenomenologists characteristically emphasize intentionality, the "aboutness" of *consciousness, and the way in which consciousness of an object presupposes a taken-for-granted "horizon of meaning" that is in the background.

philosophical theology. Philosophical inquiry into the key beliefs of theologians and concepts of *theology. In addition to such topics as arguments for and against the existence of God, philosophical theologians attempt to analyze such *divine attributes as *omnipotence, *omniscience and *eternality and also (with respect to Christianity) to assess the coherence and plausibility of such theological doctrines as the *Trinity, the *atonement and the *incarnation.

philosophy. According to William *James, philosophy is simply an unusually obstinate effort to think clearly and deeply about fundamental questions. Interestingly, what counts as philosophy is itself under dispute in philosophy. Philosophy can be identified historically in the West as the kind of activity carried on by such people as *Plato, *Aristotle, David *Hume and Immanuel *Kant. It can also be identified with reference to its fundamental questions, such as "What is knowledge?" (*epistemology), "What is reality?" (*metaphysics) and "What is good?" (*ethics). Although some would make a sharp distinction between philosophy and *theology, there is substantial overlap in the questions each treats. One way to distinguish between the two is in terms of their audiences: A thinker who is speaking to a religious community and can presuppose the authorities recognized by that community is doing theology. The same thinker addressing a broader community may be doing philosophy.

philosophy of religion. The branch of *philosophy that seeks to understand and critically evaluate the beliefs and practices of religions. Philosophers of religion debate the existence of God, the nature of religion, the possibility of life after death (and specific views about life after death such as *reincarnation and *resurrection) and many other questions raised by the great world religions.

physicalism. The doctrine that only physical realities exist and hence that there are no such entities as *God, *angels or nonphysical *souls. *Physicalism* is often used as a synonym for *materialism*, but the viewpoints are sometimes distinguished in the following way: materialists believe that only matter exists, while physicalists accept the existence of matter and energy. Some contemporary physicalists define their position in an open-ended way that refers to *science. Namely, physicalism is the theory that the ultimate constituents of reality are whatever ultimate particles or entities are accepted by physics. *See also* materialism.

Plantinga, Alvin (1932-). Leading contemporary philosopher of religion and developer of *Reformed Epistemology, along with Nicholas *Wolterstorff (who taught with Plantinga many years at Calvin College) and William *Alston. Plantinga has criticized *evidentialism in *philosophy of religion by arguing that religious beliefs in some cases may be "properly basic." This view is supported by an *epistemology that sees *knowledge as consisting of true *beliefs that are the result of properly functioning faculties, operating according to their "design plan" in a way that is directed at *truth, in the kind of environment in which they were intended to function.

Plato (c. 427-347 B.C.). Perhaps the most influential philosopher of the Western world. Plato's influence is so vast that Alfred North *Whitehead claimed that the history of Western *philosophy is merely a series of footnotes to Plato. Plato wrote in the form of dialogues, and his thinking seems to have evolved over time. He is best known for his theory of *justice, developed in the *Republic,* for his defense of the immortality of the *soul and for his theory of Forms, which posits an ideal world of universals that the material world copies or participates in. Plato also postulated one supreme or absolute Form—the Form of the Good or the One. His thinking has had a profound impact on Jewish, Christian and Islamic thought, especially as developed by *Plotinus and other *Neo-Platonist philosophers. *See also* idealism.

Plotinus (205-270). Hellenistic philosopher who developed *Plato's ideas into a philosophical and religious system that profoundly influenced early Christian writers. Plotinus emphasized the One or the Good—the supreme reality from which all else emanates and to which all will return. The One is beyond human language and discursive thought. Plotinus blended mystical and ascetic tendencies with philosophical thought. *See also* Neo-Platonism.

pluralism, religious. Descriptively, a situation characterized by a number of alternative religions and diverse perspectives on religion, with the resulting problem for adherents of each view of what attitude to take toward the other views. The contemporary world is in most places undeniably pluralistic in this sense. However, for some, the term *pluralism* has taken on a normative sense in which it implies an endorsement of this plurality and a refusal to see one religion as truer than others or superior to others in any way. *See also* relativism.

Polanyi, Michael (1891-1976). Chemist and philosopher of science who opposed *reductionism in *science. Polanyi emphasized the role of what he called "tacit knowing" in scientific discovery, which allows for the importance of *worldviews and other background assumptions, and rejected the claim that scientific work can be fully formalized. *See also* tacit knowledge.

polytheism. Belief in and veneration of more than one god or divine being. Many *pagan religions are polytheistic.

positivism. Empiricist philosophy that restricts genuine *knowledge to the so-called positive sciences that are thought to be based on the evidence of the senses. Positivists therefore tend to be skeptical of what cannot be directly observed. Nineteenth-century positivism is linked to Auguste Comte and John Stuart Mill. In the twentieth century, empiricist thought was linked with the analytical techniques of symbolic logic to form *logical positivism. *See also* empiricism.

possible worlds. Ways the actual world could have been. In the actual world I have brown hair, but perhaps there is a possible world in which I have blond hair. A set of alternatives to the actual world constitutes a possible world if it is maximal in scope—every possible state of affairs is either included or excluded. The concept of a possible world is widely used to make sense of such modal concepts as "necessity" and "possibility," and these terms figure prominently in the *ontological argument and debates about the problem of *evil. Leibniz is usually credited with first using the concept of a possible world. *See also* necessity.

postmodernism. Term used to designate a loosely connected set of trends and perspectives in various cultural and academic fields that have in common only a perceived opposition to *modernity. In philosophy, postmodernism is characterized by a suspicion of "metanarratives," an emphasis on the uncertain character of human knowing and a tendency to analyze various intellectual claims, including *Enlightenment claims about the universal character of *reason and *science, in a suspicious way as a mask for oppression and domination. The term *postmodernism* is often used syononymously with *poststructuralism* to indicate the ways in which postmodernist thinkers both reacted against and were influenced by *structuralism.

pragmatism. Philosophical movement that views ideas and *beliefs in relation to their implications for *action. A pragmatic theory of meaning should be distinguished from a pragmatic theory of *truth that rejects the idea of truth as *correspondence to reality. Pragmatism was developed in America by Charles Sanders *Peirce, William *James and John *Dewey. Pragmatism is a form of *empiricism but one that views experience as a form of dynamic interaction between the *self and the environment, rather than consisting of sensations. The movement has recently been revived and interpreted in a postmodern manner by Richard *Rorty.

prayer. Communication with God or (for some traditions) other supernatural beings and departed spirits. There are many forms of prayer, including propitiation, adoration and thanksgiving, but most philosophical discussions of prayer have focused on the problems posed by petitionary prayer, in which a person makes a request to God for some specific good. These problems include such questions as the following: Do such prayers require special divine *actions (sometimes called "interventions," though the term is misleading) in the world? Can a God who is *omniscient and perfectly *good be affected by human prayers? The solutions to such questions require thought as to why a good God would wish to employ the free actions of humans in the pursuit of his goals.

predestination. The conviction that God has in his sovereign *grace from all eternity "elected," or predestined, a body of people for *salvation. Some recent theologians have emphasized the theme that Jesus is primarily God's elect, chosen from before the foundation of the world, and that the predestination of the church must be understood in relation to being "in" or "one" with Christ. Some Calvinists hold to a "double predestination" in which God predestines those who are not part of the elect for damnation. *See also* foreknowledge, divine; free will; providence; sovereignty.

predication (analogical, univocal, equivocal). Application of descriptive terms, or "predicates," to God. If one assumes (as many do) that human language gets its meaning from its application to finite, created objects, then there is a difficulty as to how such terms can apply to God. Recently, Richard *Swinburne and William *Alston have argued that some predicates can apply univocally (with the same meaning) both to God and to creatures. Thomas *Aquinas held that positive terms can be applied to God—but only analogically. According to such a view, we do not know exactly what we mean when we say God is good, for example, but only that his goodness resembles (though exceeds) the goodness of creatures. Equivocal predication is application of the same term to God and creatures with different meanings.

presuppositionalism. An apologetic strategy often associated with Cornelius *Van Til and some of his students. The presuppositionalist emphasizes the way all human belief systems depend on unprovable basic assumptions, arguing that biblical *faith or its lack crucially shapes our presuppositions. According to such a view, common ground between the believer and unbeliever is limited or nonexistent and apologetic arguments must take the form of explorations of the unbeliever's system of thought so as to reveal contradictions within it due to its faulty presuppositions. *See also* evidentialism; Reformed Epistemology.

process theology. An approach to theology inspired by the philosophical thought of Alfred North *Whitehead and

Charles Hartshorne, with Shubert Ogden as one of its main proponents. Process theology rejects the classical picture of God as *immutable and *transcendent in favor of a God who is partly evolving with and in relation to the created world. The problem of *evil looks different in such a context. Since process theologians do not necessarily think of the natural order as created out of nothing, evil may be partly due to the recalcitrant nature of that order, in which God works persuasively along with his creatures for the *good. Process theology should be distinguished from *open theism, which questions the classical doctrine of divine *foreknowledge, though there are points of similarity between the two theologies.

prophecy. *See* argument from prophecy.

providence. The loving care and governance that God exercises over the created universe. The traditional picture of providence is one in which God, as an *omniscient, *omnipotent and perfectly *good being, has exhaustive knowledge of the past, present and future, and exercises his power so as to ensure that every event that occurs is part of his perfect plan. Some have recently questioned such a view of providence by arguing that it does not do justice to human freedom. According to a revised view, God knows all the possibilities and knows what responses he must make to ensure that his goals are achieved. The issues raised by providence are closely linked to the problems raised by *predestination and the compatibility of divine *foreknowledge and human *free will. *See also* sovereignty.

public square. A metaphorical way of referring to the "space" in which citizens of a democracy discuss and decide issues of common concern. There is much debate over the place of religion in the public square in a pluralistic democracy. Classical liberals as well as such postmodernist thinkers as Richard *Rorty argue that religion is a divisive conversation stopper that cannot offer reasons for action that are valid in the public square. Many religious believers reject this argument and claim that the supposed "neutral" standpoint of *liberalism is actually a disguised naturalistic perspective. According to such a view, the debate in the public square cannot be divorced from questions of ultimate commitments and *worldviews, and therefore religious convictions can have a positive public function in a pluralistic democracy. A more extreme position holds that the public square must be grounded in a specific religious commitment—a view that logically leads to an established form of religion.

Puritanism. A reform movement heavily influenced by Calvinism but initially part of the Church of England that had its zenith in the seventeenth century in England and North America. The stereotype of a Puritan as someone who is prudish and legalistic is quite misleading; Puritans enjoyed their beer and knew how to laugh. They were agents of cultural renewal in spheres as diverse as poetry and political philosophy, and they left a lasting imprint through the colonies founded in New England. *See also* Reformed tradition.

Q, R

rational. Quality of a *belief or *action that is in accord with *reason. There are many different forms of rationality. A person is deontologically rational when that person has fulfilled his or her rational obligations or duties (whatever those may be). (*See* deontological theory.) In this sense, a person may be rational to hold a false belief so long as the person has good reasons for the belief or has not violated any duties in forming it. Another sense of rationality relates to *truth. In this sense we may say that a belief-forming practice is rational if it is likely to result in a true belief.

rationalism. Conviction that *reason provides the best or even the only path to *truth. In *philosophy, rationalism as an epistemological theory is often contrasted with *empiricism, which emphasizes the role of sense experience in the acquisition of truth. In this context reason is understood narrowly as a faculty distinct from sensation and memory. Rationalist philosophers of this type include René *Descartes, Baruch *Spinoza and Gottfried *Leibniz. In *theology the term *rationalism* often designates a position that subordinates *revelation to human reason or rules out revelation as a source of *knowledge altogether. In this sense an empiricist can be a rationalist who gives precedence to human reason over revelation (understanding reason here in a broad sense that includes such faculties as sensation and memory). *See also* epistemology; rational.

realism. The belief that there are real entities that exist independently of human knowers. There are many types of realism, depending on the scope of the theory and the contrasting antirealist position. One type of *antirealism is *idealism. The antirealist may hold, for example, with George *Berkeley that "to be is to be perceived" and thus that physical objects do not exist if they are unperceived. (However, Berkeley can also be understood as a type of realist in that he claimed that God was always present to perceive objects and thus ground the real existence of entities unperceived by humans.) A popular contemporary form of antirealism holds that true propositions about objects in the world depend on the human concepts employed to understand those objects, and thus what is true about the world depends partly on how we humans think about that world. Realism (and its rival antirealism) can also be restricted to particular regions. Thus one can be a realist (or antirealist) about unobservable scientific entities such as quarks or abstract logical entities such as sets and numbers.

reason. The faculty or power that allows humans to think or deliberate, to see the connections between propositions and draw proper inferences. Reason can be taken in a narrow or a broad sense. In the narrow sense reason is often contrasted with sensation and memory as the power to make inferences, and truths that are known by reason are those that are known *a priori or purely by reflection. In a broader sense reason refers to the human faculties that make *knowledge possible, including memory and sensation. *See also* rational; rationalism.

redemption. One of the images or metaphors employed by the New Testament—and consequently by the church—to understand the saving work of Christ. The image is taken from the ancient institution of slavery, which allowed that a slave could be freed by being purchased (redeemed). The New Testament sees Jesus' life, death and resurrection as in some way freeing human beings from bondage to *sin by atoning for that sin. *See also* atonement; salvation.

reductionism. An attempt to explain some domain or field by showing that it can be derived from or redescribed in the language of some more basic domain or field. A physicalist, for example, may attempt a reductionistic account of the mind by showing that such entities as thoughts and perception can be reduced to physiological states of the brain. (*See* physicalism.) In *science a successful reduction requires one to show how the laws of one domain can be derived from the laws of some more fundamental domain. Reductionism often is linked to an attitude that seeks to view the explained or "reduced" field or objects as unreal.

Reformed Epistemology. An approach to questions about *knowledge and *belief inspired by the work of Alvin *Plantinga, Nicholas *Wolterstorff and William *Alston. Many of the proponents of Reformed Epistemology have links to Calvin College and are inspired by Abraham Kuyper's conception of Christian scholarship. Reformed Epistemology characteristically holds that belief in God may be "properly basic" and does not have to be based on evidence. Plantinga has developed an *epistemology that emphasizes knowledge as the result of human faculties that are functioning properly in their intended environment in accordance with a "design plan" aimed at truth.

Reformed tradition. Christian tradition specially influenced by the work of John *Calvin and his followers. The Reformed tradition is notable for its emphasis on the *sovereignty of God and the mandate of Christians to attempt to transform and redeem the various spheres of human society.

Reid, Thomas (1710-1796). Scottish philosopher widely regarded as the founder of the school of Scottish realism, or *Common Sense philosophy. Reid interpreted the philosophy of David *Hume as the skeptical outcome of the theory of ideas or mental representations begun by René *Descartes and John *Locke. He developed a form of *realism in which sensations are not the direct objects of perception but instead are the means whereby we are directly presented with objects. His thought has had a great influence on *Reformed Epistemology. Reid stressed the need to begin with an attitude of trust in our human faculties (reason, perception, memory, testimony) without insisting on *rational proof of their reliability.

reincarnation. The belief that after death a person is reborn. This doctrine was taught by *Plato and is widely held by the religions that originated in India, especially *Hinduism and *Buddhism. In these religions a person is thought to be successively reincarnated in accordance with karma (the moral principle guaranteeing that one reaps what one sows) until final purification is reached and the wheel of reincarnation is escaped. Reincarnation is most naturally understood as the rebirth of the soul in a new body, though Buddhists deny the existence of a substantial soul.

relativism. The denial of any absolute or objective standards, especially in *ethics. (*See* objectivity.) Ethical relativists can be individual relativists, who hold that what is morally right is relative to the beliefs or emotions of the individual, or they can be cultural relativists, who hold that what is morally right varies with different societies. (*See* subjectivism.) Analogously, in *epistemology relativism holds that what is true is dependent on the individual or the culture.

religious experience. Experience of God or the holy or experiences of other things that require a religious interpretation or explanation. Examples of the former would include mystical awareness of God and experiences of visions and voices in which one becomes aware of God. (*See* mysticism.) Examples of the latter might include experiencing the beautiful or sublime in nature—sunsets, mountains, births and so forth that must be seen as pointing to God. *See also* experience of God.

religious language. *See* language, religious (theories of).

resurrection. Christian doctrine that those who are redeemed in Christ are destined to live again in renewed, transformed bodies after death. The pattern for the resurrection is the resurrection of Jesus, whose body was raised from the dead on the third day after his crucifixion. The nature of resurrected bodies is mysterious, but the church has traditionally taught that there will be both continuity and discontinuity between our current earthly bodies and our "spiritual" resurrection bodies.

retribution. Receiving what one deserves; in particular, the punishment of evil. Christianity has traditionally held a doctrine of a final *judgment in which God will judge all people on the basis of their *actions on earth. The church also holds that God has judged *sin through the sufferings and death of Jesus (understood as making propitiation for human sins, thus making it possible for humans to face God's judgment without terror). A retributive theory of punishment is one that views punishment not merely as a deterrent or an incentive to reform but as something that a wrongdoer deserves. *See also* justice.

revelation. What God has made known about himself and the process by which this insight is given. Most theologians have distinguished between the *general revelation of God given in nature and quasiuniversal human experiences (such as our sense of dependence) and special revelations given to and through specific individuals in history, particularly the prophets and Jesus himself—God's supreme revelation.

Ricoeur, Paul (1913-). French Protestant philosopher who has taught at the University of Paris and the Divinity School of the University of Chicago. Ricoeur has been one of the leaders in the development of philosophical hermeneutics rooted in the phenomenological method of Edmund *Husserl, which stresses the description of lived experience. While emphasizing the need for the "hermeneutics of suspicion" exemplified in Sigmund *Freud, Karl *Marx and Friedrich *Nietzsche, Ricoeur holds out the possibility of a "second naiveté" that goes beyond suspicion. Ricoeur has worked on the "symbolism of evil," the philosophy of literature and the philosophy of action in addition to the *philosophy of religion.

Romanticism. Philosophical and literary movement of the late eighteenth and early nineteenth centuries that emphasized spontaneous feeling and individual freedom in reaction against the *rationalism of the *Enlightenment. In *theology Romanticism had significant influence on Friedrich *Schleiermacher.

Rorty, Richard (1931-). Leading American proponent of postmodern philosophy. (*See* postmodernism.) Trained in *analytic philosophy, Rorty argues that the collapse of *foundationalism should lead us to reject traditional philosophical views of *truth as accurate representations of reality in favor of the *pragmatism of John *Dewey. According to Rorty, the philosopher should take an ironical perspective that recognizes no foundation for the views defended other than our own linguistic practices and preferences. Philosophy is a persuasive and rhetorical endeavor that cannot be sharply distinguished from literature.

Rousseau, Jean Jacques (1712-1778). French philosopher born in Switzerland whose influence on political theory and theories of education has been enormous. Rousseau saw human individuals as naturally good but corrupted by education and society. His political theory stresses individual freedom but ultimately subordinates the individual to the general will, which is established by a social contract allowing individuals to live together as citizens. Rousseau's ideas influenced the French Revolution and helped shape the development of *Romanticism.

Russell, Bertrand (1872-1970). British logician and advocate of social causes who was one of the founding fathers of *analytic philosophy. With Alfred North *Whitehead, Russell wrote *Principia Mathematica*, which attempts to show that the whole of mathematics can be derived from logic. Though Russell frequently changed his philosophical positions, he generally held to some form of *realism, regarded *science as the paradigm of human *knowledge and rejected religion and traditional sexual morality.

S

salvation. Christian term for God's work in delivering human beings from the power of *sin and the devil through the life, death and resurrection of Jesus. In a broader sense *salvation* may refer to God's restoration of the whole of the created order to its intended purposes. *See also* atonement; conversion; redemption.

Sartre, Jean Paul (1905-1980). French writer and philosopher, most famous for his development of *existentialism in the period following World War II. The heart of Sartre's philosophy is his affirmation of individual freedom and responsibility. Though we do not create our situation, we are always free to negate and interpret our situation and we are ultimately responsible for what we become. Because of his *atheism, Sartre insisted that there is no ideal realm of values independent of human choice, but rather we are "forlorn" as we face an "absurd" world.

Schaeffer, Francis (1912-1984). Evangelical thinker, writer and speaker who had a dramatic impact on young evangelicals in the 1960s and 1970s. Schaeffer was a Bible Presbyterian minister who went to Switzerland as a missionary in 1948. With his wife, Edith, he developed L'Abri—a ministry to young people from Europe and North America. Such books as *The God Who Is There* and *Escape from Reason,* developed from his lectures, popularized his view that Western culture had descended into irrationalism as a consequence of its rejection of biblical Christianity. Schaeffer's analysis of history was wide-ranging, covering fields as diverse as art, philosophy and politics. In his later years he increasingly emphasized the evils of abortion.

Schleiermacher, Friedrich (1768-1834). Influential developer of liberal Protestant theology. Schleiermacher viewed the foundation of *theology to be the human experience of dependence rather than the Bible, which he viewed as a valuable record of such experiences. Influenced by *Romanticism, Schleiermacher attempted to defend religion against its "cultured despisers" by reaching an accommodation with modern culture. *See also* liberalism (theological).

Scholasticism. The medieval philosophical and theological tradition in which Greek philosophy was synthesized with the Bible and teachings of the church fathers. Leading figures included *Anselm, Thomas *Aquinas, John *Duns Scotus and William of *Ockham. In the period after the Reformation a number of theologians known as Protestant scholastics attempted to systematize Lutheran and Calvinist thought in ways that resembled the work of the medieval Scholastics in both style and content.

science. The systematic, empirically based search for *knowledge, from the Latin term for knowledge, *scientia.* Specific disciplines that focus on a particular kind of reality are also called sciences, and the sciences thus conceived are frequently classified as either natural sciences (biology, chemistry, physics, geology) or social or human sciences (economics, sociology, politcal science, psychology, anthropology). In Germany and much of Europe the corresponding terms for science (such as *Wissenschaft*) have a broader sense and refer to any organized pattern of academic research, including such disciplines as philosophy and literary criticism. Much discussion of religious belief since the seventeenth century has focused on alleged and real tensions between science and religious beliefs, with the biological *theory of evolution being a particular flash point in the late nineteenth and twentieth centuries.

scientism. The conviction that scientific knowledge, particularly that derived from the natural *sciences, is the highest or even only form of *knowledge. Scientism thus depreciates the possibility that ultimate truth can be derived from such areas as moral, aesthetic and religious experience, and it typically rejects the idea that truth can be derived from a *special *revelation.

Scotus, John Duns. *See* Duns Scotus, John.

secularism. A belief system, attitude or style of life that denies or ignores the reality of God. Derived from a term that means "worldly," secularism (and its articulate philosophical expression, secular humanism) focuses on the natural order of things as the only reality. Increasingly, however, secularism can be viewed as an attitude that even affects people who claim to believe in God and the supernatural. Much in modern culture pressures people to live in such a way that God is marginal and insignificant to their daily existence. *See also* humanism.

self. The "I" that is the seat of conscious reflection and source of intentional activity, often understood as identical to the *soul. There is much philosophical debate about the nature of the self and its relation to the body. Can a person survive the death of the body? To think of a person as a self is to focus specially on the subjective, interior dimensions of a person's being—I am aware of myself as a self in ways that I cannot be aware of others. There is also much debate about the freedom and responsibility of the self. Can a conscious self transcend to any degree the causal forces that have shaped the self? *See also* identity, personal; personhood.

sexuality. The dimension of humans and animals that is grounded in the distinction between maleness and femaleness. In contemporary philosophy many thinkers view sexuality as at least partly a cultural construction and thus use the term *gender* for aspects of humanness that reflect being male and female to indicate the lack of biological determination. *Postmodern philosophers take *gender, so conceived, to be an important dimension of the human self that shapes *philosophy and *theology profoundly, as well as human culture generally, since much traditional thought reflects an unconscious male bias. *See also* patriarchy, matriarchy.

sign. An entity that carries information, particularly about something beyond itself. Semiotics, or the theory of signs, includes three areas of study: (1) syntax looks at the relations signs have to each other; (2) semantics looks at the relations between signs and what signs signify; and (3) pragmatics looks at the ways signs are used. In Paul *Tillich's theology a sign is distinguished (somewhat idiosyncratically) from a symbol in that a symbol is said to participate in or have some kind of internal relation to that which it signifies.

simplicity. Two senses: (1) hard-to-describe but desirable lack of complexity in scientific theories; (2) the *divine attribute of being completely unified and having no distinct parts. In philosophy of science, it is widely accepted that scientists choose among a plurality of theories equally consistent with the facts on the basis of simplicity, though there is little agreement as to why simplicity should be a criterion of *truth or even what counts as simplicity. The criterion of simplicity is also employed in other fields epistemologically. For example, some theologians argue that thinking of God's knowledge and power as infinite is preferable because it is simpler than the attribution of some finite, but arbitrary, amount of power and knowledge to God. In theology simplicity is one of the more mysterious of the properties attributed to God by the medieval Scholastics, since it seems to imply that no distinction can be drawn between God's existence and his essence, between his will and his intellect, or indeed among any of his properties.

sin. That fundamental defect or missing of the mark that results when humans fail to trustingly center their lives on God. Sin can be viewed both as a state in which humans are alienated from God and as *actions that stem from an unfaithful heart and thus go against God's will. In addition, sin can be understood both as a reality within individuals and as a factor shaping social structures. *See also* Fall, the.

skepticism. The denial of genuine human *knowledge. Skepticism about particular fields (such as parapsychology) should be distinguished from general or universal skepticism. In ancient times skepticism (sometimes called Pyrrhonism) was defended by such philosophers as Sextus Empiricus. The ancient skeptics recommended their view as a way of obtaining *ataraxia* (peace of mind). Skepticism in modern philosophy is sometimes regarded as a methodological tool, as in the philosophy of René *Descartes. Many attempts have been made by modern philosophers to refute skeptical arguments that imply that it is not possible to know the external world, that other people have minds or that induction can be rationally justified. Some themes in *postmodern and *antirealist contemporary philosophy are similar to those of skeptics.

Smith, Wilfred Cantwell (1916-2000). One of the preeminent advocates of pluralistic views toward the world religions. Though Smith was a former Christian missionary to India, he opposed attempts to convert adherents of one major religion to another, arguing that all of these religions represent alternative paths to God. Smith did not look on religions as abstract sets of doctrines but as practices that "become true" in the lives of believers. *See also* pluralism, religious.

social trinitarianism. Theories of the *Trinity inspired by some of the Greek church fathers that emphasize the distinctness of the three persons of the Trinity and understand the oneness of the Trinity as the unity of a community. (*See* Cappadocian fathers.) The danger in such a view is that it will slide into tritheism, a belief in three gods.

Socrates (c. 470-399 B.C.). One of the most important Greek philosophers, executed by the Athenians on the charge of corrupting youth with his philosophy and undermining the religion of the city by refusing to recognize its gods and introducing new ones. Socrates wrote nothing himself, but he has exercised an incalculable influence on the history of philosophy through his depiction by *Plato in a series of dialogues. In daily conversations with Athenians, Socrates challenged and questioned prevailing wisdom, holding that he was wiser than his contemporaries only in recognizing that he knew nothing. True wisdom, said Socrates, was a possession of the gods. He regarded his philosophical work as a divine calling and refused to cease his activity even to save his life. The critical Socrates is regarded as a hero by contemporary secular philosophy, but the religious Socrates (who apparently heard voices and was confident that "nothing can harm a good man in life and death" because "the gods are not indifferent to his fortunes") is not so widely hailed.

sola fides. Latin for "faith alone." This phrase refers to the Reformation doctrine that *salvation is completely the result of *faith and is in no way the outcome of good works.

sola gratia. Latin for "grace alone." This phrase refers to the Reformation conviction that *salvation is by God's *grace alone and that even saving *faith is due to the gracious activity of God and cannot be viewed as a meritorious human achievement.

sola Scriptura. Latin for "Scripture alone." This phrase refers to the Reformation conviction that only the Bible can serve as an ultimate *authority for the church. Strictly speaking, the Reformers did not rule out church *tradition as having any value, but they insisted that it be subordinate to the teachings of Scripture.

solipsism. The doctrine that a person has a direct awareness only of his or her own conscious states and is in some way cut off from the reality of other things. The extreme form of solipsism is ontological solipsism, which denies the reality of anything outside one's own mind. The denials that a person can know the external world or other minds can be viewed as forms of epistemological solipsism. *See also* perception.

soul. A person understood as a conscious, responsible being. Many philosophers from *Plato onward, as well as many Christian theologians, have believed that the soul in this sense is an immaterial or spiritual entity that is capable of being separated from the body at death and (for Plato) reincarnated or (for Christians) resurrected or reembodied at a later time. Many contemporary philosophers have rejected this dualistic picture of the human soul in favor of *materialism. Surprisingly, many theologians agree, holding that this dualistic picture is more Greek than biblical, though it is unclear how a materialistic view can deal with Christian teachings about life after death, particularly during the intermediate state between death and resurrection. *See also* dualism; reincarnation; resurrection.

sovereignty. The possession of ultimate authority and power. In political theory the state is often regarded as sovereign, while in *theology, sovereignty is a characteristic of the all-powerful, all-knowing Creator, who governs the universe for his own purposes. The concept of divine sovereignty is particularly emphasized by Augustinian and Reformed (Calvinist) thinkers. *See also* divine attributes; Reformed tradition.

special revelation. Revelation given by God through particular persons, experiences, writings or historical events. Special revelation is normally distinguished from *general revelation.

Spinoza, Baruch (1632-1677). One of the most important philosophers of the rationalist tradition, Spinoza was expelled from the Jewish synagogue in Amsterdam for his unorthodox views. (*See* rationalism.) Spinoza was a monist who held that fundamentally only one substance exists, known through its two attributes of mind and extension and correctly designated as God or Nature. (*See* monism; pantheism.) When we understand the nature of God, we understand that all that happens does so with *necessity. True *happiness consists in the intellectual love of God when we see the world under the aspect of eternity and accept all that happens as ultimately good. Spinoza believed that philosophy should be done in a geometric method involving self-evident postulates and definitions from which theorems can be proved.

Stoicism. An influential philosophy in ancient Greece and in the Roman world that emphasized a person's control over the emotions. Founded by Zeno of Citium (334-262 B.C.; not to be confused with Zeno the Eleatic, famous for his paradoxes), Stoicism evolved over time, with three periods usually distinguished: Early Stoicism, Middle Stoicism and Roman Stoicism. Most surviving Stoic writings come from the last period, with the slave Epictetus and the emperor Marcus Aurelius being two of the most famous Stoics. Stoicism was characterized by a conviction that the universe has a rational structure and that whatever happens does so with necessity. True virtue requires an acceptance of external events; the virtuous person lives in accordance with the reason that shapes the universe and gains contentment by an attitude of indifference to the external goods and evils that most people desire and fear.

Strauss, David Friedrich (1808-1874). Most famous as the author of *The Life of Jesus* (1835), a pioneering and influential work in German higher biblical criticism. Educated at Tübingen, Strauss was the first to say in a forthright manner that the supernatural aspects of the gospel narratives were nonhistorical myth. He was also one of the first to argue that seeing the texts as myth allows us to grasp their true, metaphysical meaning. *See also* liberalism (theological).

structuralism. An interdisciplinary movement with its origins in linguistics and French philosophy that emphasizes the way in which the meanings of symbols are determined by their relationships to other symbols in a system. Structuralists see language and other human activities (including religious rituals) as reflecting deep, universal structures often expressed in myth. *See also* postmodernism; sign.

subjectivism. Philosophy or life perspective that attempts to view what is normally thought to be objectively true or false as subjective. In *ethics, emotivism, which views ethical judgments as expressions of subjective emotions, is an example of subjectivism. Subjectivism is in effect a type of individual *relativism. *See also* objectivity.

substance. In philosophy, that which exists independently as an objective entity. A substance, such as a dog, is thus distinguished from a property, such as the dog's color, which must be possessed or owned by a substance. Although the term *substance* is derived from the Latin term *substantia*, various Greek and Latin terms have been translated as *substance*, and this has created much confusion in theology. The doctrine of the *Trinity is generally formulated as the belief that God exists in three persons but as only one substance. Some Christian philosophers have argued that God cannot be viewed as a substance because the term is either too static in character or is applied primarily to finite creatures. Others reject the category altogether on the grounds that nothing can exist that is truly independent of God. But this latter view verges dangerously close to Baruch *Spinoza's *pantheism.

sufficient reason, principle of. The claim that there must be an explanation for every positive fact, some reason why that fact obtains rather than not obtaining. This principle is generally attributed to Gottfried *Leibniz, for whom it took the form of the assumption that God has a sufficient reason for every choice he has made. The principle, or some variation on it, often plays a key role in *cosmological arguments for the existence of God, who is argued to be the only adequate explanation for the existence of the finite universe. Those who deny the principle of sufficient reason are committed to the claim that some facts obtain for no reason, and thus that there is a surd (nonrational) element to the universe.

supererogation. Moral *actions that go beyond what is required by duty, especially those actions that are commendable and indicative of superior *character. Some Protestants have been critical of the idea of supererogation on the grounds that humans never fully realize their moral duties, much less exceed them. But there is a clear sense in which certain actions—for example, deciding to donate a kidney to a stranger—go beyond what is required by duty and seem to express a high degree of moral character. *See also* ethics; morality.

Swinburne, Richard (1934-). One of the preeminent philosophers of religion in the *analytic philosophy tradition. Swinburne, who holds a chair at Oxford University, made his reputation with a trilogy in which he first defended the coherence of *theism, then argued the probability of God's existence and finally argued for the reasonableness of Christian *belief. He has since treated a number of topics of special relevance to Christianity, including the *Trinity, the *atonement and *revelation. Swinburne's work is notable for its rigor and reliance on inductive probability.

symbol. *See* sign.

T

tacit knowledge. A term used by philosopher of science Michael *Polanyi to describe the kind of background *knowledge that people possess but may be unable to articulate. Polanyi argued that this kind of knowledge, which is often ignored by philosophers, is essential to *science and many other fields. Tacit knowledge is usually gained through participation in a community, and it is often linked to "knowing how" as opposed to "knowing that."

Taoism. An ancient philosophical and religious *worldview developed in China. The term derives from the Chinese word *tao*, meaning "the way." Taoists believe that there is an underlying metaphysical and ethical structure to the cosmos and that humans who understand this can order their lives rightly. However, this structure, or *tao*, is *ineffable, and thus our knowledge of it is not propositional in character. The most famous Taoist philosophers were Chuang-tzu and Lao-tzu.

teleological argument. An argument for the existence of God that takes as its starting point the purposive (teleological) character of the universe. The argument is often termed "the argument from design" and comes in many different versions. This argument was quite popular in the eighteenth and early nineteenth centuries, but many atheists believe it has been discredited by *Darwinism. Philosophers of religion such as Richard *Swinburne, however, have developed versions of the argument that are compatible with Darwinism. *See also* intelligent design; theistic arguments.

Tertullian (c. 160-230). One of the most important of the early church fathers. Tertullian wrote in Latin and thus had a particularly strong influence on the Western church. Tertullian is perhaps best known for his polemical attitude toward Greek *philosophy, expressed in the memorable question "What has Athens to do with Jerusalem?" He wrote many important apologetic and theological works, though he drifted into the heresy of Montanism at the end of his life.

theism. The view that God, understood as one infinite, all-powerful, all-knowing, completely good person, exists and has created the universe. Equivalent to monotheism. *See also* atheism; pantheism; panentheism; polytheism.

theistic arguments. Arguments for the existence of God, as God is understood by theists. (*See* theism.) Such arguments may be intended as proofs or merely as arguments that confirm or increase the probability or plausibility of belief that God exists. Some of the most important theistic arguments include the *ontological argument, the *cosmological argument, the *teleological argument and the *moral argument.

theistic attributes. *See* attributes of God.

theodicy. An answer to the problem of *evil that attempts to "justify the ways of God to man" by explaining God's reasons for allowing evil. Two of the more important theodicies are the "soul-making theodicy," which argues that God allows evil so as to make it possible for humans to develop certain desirable virtues, and the "free will theodicy," which argues that God had to allow for the possibility of evil if he wished to give humans (and angelic beings) *free will. Theodicies are often distinguished from defenses, which argue that it is reasonable to believe that God has reasons for allowing evil even if we do not know what those reasons are.

theology. The ordered, systematic study of *God and of God's relations to his creatures. There are many different types of theology. *Philosophical theology attempts to discern what can be known about God without presupposing any particular *revelation or church teaching as authoritative. Biblical theology attempts to develop theology out of the study of biblical texts, and it comes in more specific forms, such as New Testament theology, Pauline theology, Markan theology and so on. Systematic theology draws on both biblical theology and philosophical theology to develop a comprehensive account of God and his relations to the world. Dogmatic theology attempts to do theology from the perspective of the teachings (or *dogmas) of the church or some specific church.

Thomism. Philosophical views inspired by Thomas *Aquinas, who synthesized Christian thought with Aristotelian philosophy. (*See* Aristotle.) Thomism is strongest among Roman Catholic thinkers and is characterized by a confidence in *natural theology, though it also includes a strong affirmation that some Christian truths can only be believed on the basis of faith in a *special *revelation. In general the Thomistic tradition believes that "grace presupposes nature and perfects it." Twentieth-century neo-Thomists included Etienne Gilson and Jacques Maritain.

Tillich, Paul (1886-1965). One of the most important Protestant theologians of the twentieth century. Tillich viewed God as "the ground of Being" and argued that we must go beyond the traditional God of *theism (a particular conscious agent capable of action and relationship). Faith, for Tillich, was a state of "ultimate concern," and he argued that a healthy faith demands an infinite object. When faith is directed to finite objects, we get such forms of idolatry as nationalism and racism.

time. The relation that successive events in the universe have to each other. It seems impossible to describe the nature of this relation without employing some notion such as "before and after." This confirms *Augustine's famous comment that he knows what time is until someone asks him to define it. Philosophers have disagreed vigorously about the reality of "tense" and "becoming." Time is experienced by us as a series of "nows" that quickly become past and that anticipate future "nows." However, many philosophers have argued that temporal events are simply an ordered sequence (the "B series") and that what might be called "becoming" is only an appearance. Theologians have disagreed over the relation of God to time, with the majority of traditional theologians holding that God is eternal in the sense of being timeless. *See also* eternity/

everlasting; timelessness.

timelessness. One way of understanding the eternality of God. Those who accept a strong view of divine *immutability typically think of God as a being who completely transcends *time and for whom there is no "before and after," though God knows the temporal relations all events have to each other. The contrary view thinks of God as everlasting and thus sharing in the temporality of creation in some way. *See also* eternity/everlasting.

tolerance. A trait regarded as one of the chief *virtues by contemporary Western societies. Tolerance is often confused with a relativistic refusal to criticize another view or make any substantive value judgments. (*See* relativism.) However, logically, tolerance is consistent with an attitude of strong disagreement and even disapproval. There are many views I may tolerate (in the sense that I think people should be allowed to hold them) that I think are mistaken or harmful. Tolerance is also sometimes confused with respect, but the two attitudes are distinct. I may respect a committed political rebel even though I do not tolerate his behavior. I may tolerate people whom I do not respect at all.

Torrance, Thomas F. (1913-). An important contemporary Scottish theologian. Torrance is both a student and an interpreter of Karl *Barth. Strongly influenced by the Greek church fathers and by John *Calvin, Torrance has been a leader in theological reflection on *science and scientific method. He conceives of theological doctrines such as the *Trinity as analogous to scientific constructs that open an imaginative door into a reality that cannot be fully understood.

tradition. A body of wisdom or received doctrines passed down and developed by a historical community. From a term that means something "handed over," tradition originally meant the Scriptures and later the creeds passed down by the Jewish people and then (in Christianity) the church. The term now is understood more broadly as referring to any faith passed down by a community, so that one may speak of Hindu traditions as well as specific forms of Christian tradition, such as the *Reformed tradition. The relative *authority of the traditions of the church as expressed in creeds and councils, when compared with the Scriptures, was an issue during the Reformation, since the Reformers posited that the Bible has a higher authority than tradition. *See also sola Scriptura.*

transcendence. That which is higher than or surpasses other things. What is transcendent is thus relative to what is transcended. God is conceived by traditional theologians as being transcendent with respect to the created universe, meaning that he is outside the universe and that no part of the universe is identical to him or a part of him. To think of God as transcendent with respect to *time is to conceive him as *timeless. Immanuel *Kant believed that God was transcendent in the sense of being beyond the possibility of any human experience. Theologians have usually balanced an emphasis on God's transcendence with an emphasis on God's immanence within the created world as embodied in his knowledge of and action within that world. In the twentieth century some process theologians and feminist theologians criticized the claim that God is transcendent in favor of a view that sees God and the world as intimately united. *See also* feminism; process theology.

transcendental argument. An argument that takes some phenomenon as undeniable and makes claims about what must be true *a priori for this to be the case. A classical example is Immanuel *Kant's transcendental argument, in which he took the validity of scientific knowledge as given and argued that *science is possible only if we assume that such *knowledge is grounded in the a priori forms of intuition provided by the human mind (space and time) and in the a priori *categories provided by the human understanding, such as causality and *substance.

Transcendentalism. Unorthodox religious movement in nineteenth-century New England influenced by *Romanticism and emphasizing *a priori intuition. Ralph Waldo Emerson and Henry David Thoreau, the most famous Transcendentalists, were both avid readers of Samuel Taylor Coleridge but agreed on little between themselves.

transcendentals. In classical philosophy, the universal predicates, such as unity, being, and goodness, that are supposed to apply to all things and transcend any scheme of classification such as that provided by *Aristotle's *categories. Whatever exists of whatever type must be conceived as being one, being good, having existence and so on.

transubstantiation. The theory of the Eucharist officially taught by the Roman Catholic Church. According to this view, during Communion the substance or essence of the bread and wine is miraculously transformed into the body and blood of Christ, even though the "accidents" (outward appearances) of the bread and wine remain the same.

Trinity. The Christian understanding of *God as one in essence though consisting of three distinct persons: Father, Son and Holy Spirit. The seeds of the doctrine lie in the New Testament witness that God reveals himself in three forms: as the Father who is the source of all things, as the divine Word who came in flesh to reveal the Father and redeem the fallen race, and as the Spirit who gives life and unity to the church and witnesses to the Father and divine Word. The theological terminology used by the church to express the doctrine has shifted meaning over time. The Greek fathers spoke of three *hypostases* (entities) in one *ousia* (being or substance), which became in Latin three *personae* in one *substantia.* The term for a person, however, in both Greek and Latin, did not carry the strong sense of individual self-consciousness found in the contemporary term.

truth. That which corresponds to or adequately expresses what is real. Most philosophers have conceived of truth solely as a property of propositions. The most common account of propositional truth is the *correspondence theory, which holds that a proposition is true if and only if it corresponds to the way things are. Rival accounts include the coherence theory, which views truth as the property of a proposition that is part of the most coherent system of propositions, and the pragmatic theory, which defines true propositions in terms of their usefulness in making predictions and dealing with reality. Ordinary language and the Bible use the term *truth* more broadly. Thus we speak of true friendship and truth in a relationship. It is in this sense that Jesus claims, in the Gospels, that his own life is the truth (a claim that Søren *Kierkegaard attempted to illuminate through his famous statement that truth is "subjectivity" or "inwardness"—that inner passion that directs a person's life toward that which is genuine). *See also* coherentism; pragmatism; subjectivism.

U

universalism. The belief that all persons will eventually be saved and thus that no one will be eternally lost. Some universalists hold that all will be saved because of the work of Christ, but some deny the unique deity of Christ and necessity of his work for *salvation in favor of a pluralistic view that sees the world's religions as equally valid. Universalism should not be confused with the view that it is possible that *some* who do not have conscious faith in Christ in this life may be saved. It also should be distinguished from annihilationism, which holds that those who are eternally lost cease to exist altogether.

univocal. Adjective describing the status of a term that is used in the same sense throughout the course of an argument or in the same sense when applied to both God and finite objects. *See also* analogical predication; equivocal; predication (analogical, univocal, equivocal).

utilitarianism. The ethical theory, held by such thinkers as Jeremy Bentham and John Stuart Mill, asserting that moral rightness is determined by what leads to the greatest good for the greatest number of people. (*See* ethics; good, the.) Traditional utilitarians identify the greatest good with *happiness and define happiness in terms of pleasure and the absence of *pain, while "ideal" utilitarians are willing to include other goods than pleasure in their calculation of benefits. The traditional view is held by many animal rights advocates, who argue that the pleasures and pains of animals have great moral weight (equal to humans, in some cases). Act utilitarians hold that what is morally right is determined by the consequences of particular acts, while rule utilitarians hold that *morality is a matter of conforming to rules or principles and that the right set of principles consists of those that would, if followed, lead to the greatest good for the greatest number. *See also* consequentialism.

V

Van Til, Cornelius (1896-1987). Reformed theologian, born in the Netherlands and educated at Calvin College and Seminary and Princeton Theological Seminary, who had a profound influence on many students at Westminster Seminary. Van Til defended a *presuppositionalism denying that the issue between Christianity and its rivals can be decided by an appeal to agreed-upon facts. Instead he argued that every belief system is grounded in an ultimate presupposition, Christianity being grounded in the self-attesting *revelation of the triune God. Non-Christian views must be critiqued by pointing out the internal contradictions that arise from their inadequate presuppositions. *See also* evidentialism; Reformed Epistemology.

verification theory of meaning. Theory held by logical positivists, summarized in the slogan "the meaning of a proposition is its method of verification." *Logical positivism, popularized in English by A. J. Ayer, held that all propositions that have cognitive meaning (are either true or false) are either analytic (true or false solely because of the meaning of the terms) or else verifiable by sense experience. The heart of the view is the claim that all nonanalytic propositions are empirically verifiable. The positivists believed this would show that religious and metaphysical propositions were meaningless. Unfortunately for the positivists, it was soon noticed that the verification theory of meaning does not pass its own test for meaningfulness: it does not seem to be true by definition, and it is not empirically verifiable. It also was discovered that many propositions of science were not directly verifiable. But when the theory was weakened to allow such propositions meaning, it was easily shown that theological and metaphysical propositions were also meaningful on the weaker criterion. *See also* language, religious (theories of).

virtue. A disposition or *character trait that is itself an excellence or *good or that tends to lead to what is good, with moral virtues being those excellences that foster human flourishing. In ancient and medieval philosophy ethical thinking centered on the virtues—what they are, how they are related and how they are to be achieved. The medievals accepted the cardinal virtues of the ancient world (wisdom, justice, courage, temperance) and added to them the three principal Christian virtues (faith, hope and love). Both ancient and medieval thinkers tied their account of the virtues as leading to human flourishing to accounts of human nature. Recent ethical theory has seen a rediscovery of the importance of the virtues and the development of virtue theory, which holds that concepts of the virtues are basic to *ethics and not reducible to claims about moral duties or what is impersonally valuable.

voluntarism. A philosophical view that makes a choice of the will to be an essential aspect of the understanding of some phenomena. Thus voluntarism with respect to beliefs is the claim that beliefs are chosen or willed. Theological voluntarism holds that God's will is in some way superior to or independent of his intellect. For example, a theological voluntarist might say that what is good is good because God wills it, and God's understanding of goodness is thus dependent on his willing. A weak sense of voluntarism holds that the human will is not determined by the intellect; thus a person does not necessarily choose what the understanding sees as the best option.

W

wager argument. An argument developed by Blaise *Pascal that urges an unbeliever to attempt to develop *faith in God even if the evidence for God's existence is not decisive. Pascal compared belief and unbelief in God to a wager and pointed out the potential gains and losses each bet holds. If some bet on God and are wrong, they will lose only the paltry pleasure from some sins in this life that they might have enjoyed. If others bet on God and are right, however, they stand to gain eternal bliss. The potential gains and losses are thus staggeringly disproportionate, and Pascal urged the unbeliever to pray, attend Mass and do whatever else may be necessary to develop faith.

Weil, Simone (1909-1943). French religious philosopher and writer who applied Christian insights to the problem of alienated labor. Weil developed a *kenotic understanding of the *incarnation of Jesus that leads to a view of God himself as fundamentally revealed through self-emptying. Those who follow Christ can give meaning to human suffering by renouncing claims of power and entering into the afflictions of their fellow creatures.

Westphal, Merold (1940-). A leading contemporary Christian philosopher who has probably done more than any other thinker to relate Christian ideas to postmodern thought. (*See* postmodernism.) Distinguished for his work on G. W. F. *Hegel and Søren *Kierkegaard, Westphal wrote *Suspicion and Faith: The Religious Uses of Modern Atheism,* in which he shows how Christians can appropriate some of the critiques of Karl *Marx, Sigmund *Freud and Friedrich *Nietzsche.

Whitehead, Alfred North (1861-1947). English logician, mathematician and philosopher, whose later metaphysical work provided the inspiration for *process theology. Whitehead first achieved fame as the coauthor, with Bertrand *Russell, of *Principia Mathematica,* one of the seminal works of modern symbolic logic. Whitehead's later metaphysical work attempts to reject the notion of *substance as philosophically basic by taking organically related events as basic to *ontology. God functions in this system not as a personal agent but more as the ground of possibilities and alluring ideal that leads to their actualization.

Wicca. A religion that centers on witchcraft and the revival of pagan practices. Wiccans deny that their religion involves the worship of Satan and see themselves as fostering a religion that is close to nature and affirmative of such elements of *paganism as the worship of "the goddess"—a practice that is linked by Wiccans to radical forms of feminist thought. *See also* feminism.

will to believe. William *James's term for a religious choice that is justified not by evidence but by the pragmatic or life-enhancing character of the option. James held that the will to believe can only be rightly exercised when a person is choosing between two possibilities in a situation where the option is "living," "forced" and "momentous." A living option is one where both possibilities are psychologically credible (there is enough evidence to make belief possible). A forced option is one where, practically, one must have some kind of belief, because logically there are only two options and each has implications for how one must live. A momentous option is one where the life consequences of the choice are significant. *See also* belief; pragmatism.

Wittgenstein, Ludwig (1889-1951). Austrian-born philosopher who had his greatest impact on Anglo-American philosophy. Early in his career Wittgenstein expounded a picture theory of meaning that regarded complex propositions as functions of "atomic propositions" that pictured "atomic facts." According to this view, ethical and religious propositions belong to "the mystical," which cannot be expressed in language. The later Wittgenstein developed a more flexible theory of language that emphasized how meaning is a function of use. Words are used in many different contexts as part of "language games," and meaning must be situated with reference to that language game and the form of life in which the game has its home. Some of the later Wittgenstein's thoughts on religion have been developed into Wittgensteinian *fideism, which emphasizes the autonomy of the religious language game and denies the need for any justification of religious belief. In the thought of some of its proponents, however, this Wittgensteinian view is linked to religious *antirealism, in which religious propositions do not state facts that can be objectively true or false. *See also* analytic philosophy; language, religious (theories of).

Wolterstorff, Nicholas (1932-). Prominent contemporary Christian philosopher, one of the founders of *Reformed Epistemology, who taught with Alvin *Plantinga at Calvin College before accepting a chair at Yale Divinity School. In addition to his work on *epistemology Wolterstorff has written important works on aesthetics, on the theory of universals and on *revelation. He is known to many as the author of the personal and poignant *Lament for a Son*.

worldview. Comprehensive set of basic or ultimate beliefs that fit together in a consistent or coherent manner. A full worldview would include answers to the following questions and more: What kinds of realities are there, and what is ultimately real? What explanation can be given of reality? What is *knowledge, and how do we gain it? What is it to have a reasonable or justified *belief? What is *the good, what is the good life for a human person and how does a person achieve such a life? What is *beauty, and how is it related to reality and goodness?

worship. The adoration and praise of *God, ascribing to him the value and worth that is due to him. Worship includes a recognition of one's own dependence on God and is inspired by God's greatness as well as God's goodness as extended to oneself and others. Theologians typically claim that God does not require worship from humans because of any need to be praised on his part but because worship deepens a relation to God on our part and leads to our own fulfillment.

X, Y, Z

Zen Buddhism. A form of *Buddhism that originated in China and then spread to Japan. Zen Buddhism is a type of Mahayana Buddhism which holds out the possibility that individuals can attain the status of Buddhahood through following various esoteric teachings and exercises. The teachings of Zen do not lend themselves to straightforward explanation, as its adherents hold that the path to *enlightenment cannot be discursively described.

Zoroastrianism. A religion from ancient Persia (Iran) that dominated that region prior to the coming of Islam but is today a small minority faith. Named for the prophet Zoroaster (or Zarathustra), whose dates are unknown, Zoroastrianism became the official religion of Persia from the third century B.C. until the seventh century A.D. It is characterized by a *dualism in which Ahura Mazda, the god of light and goodness, struggles to overcome a powerful evil spirit, although contemporary Zoroastrians claim that they are monotheists and do not necessarily see the physical world as bad, as in the ontological dualism of *Manichaeism.